THE FUTURE OF INCLUSIVE FINANCE

3RD ASIA FINANCE FORUM CONFERENCE PROCEEDINGS

OCTOBER 2020

ASIAN DEVELOPMENT BANK

CONTENTS

MAIN FORUM

INTRODUCTION

There are 1.7 billion people who are outside of the formal banking and financial system, more than half of whom are in Asia and the Pacific. They struggle with high fees and risky systems to undertake even simple financial transactions.

In order to improve the lives of the poorest and most vulnerable, it is crucial to connect these marginalized populations with the broader economy. As we have entered the Fourth Industrial Revolution, the use of digital technology in financial services can offer new ways to bring them out of financial darkness. The Third Asia Finance Forum held on 6–7 November 2019 at the ADB headquarters envisioned the future of inclusive finance by discussing how new technologies like artificial intelligence, big data, and blockchain, as well as the rapid expansion of mobile phone banking, are helping to bring financial services to unbanked communities. These digital technologies can boost financial inclusion by expanding how people financially transact beyond traditional banking. Efforts in several specific areas can make a big difference, including identification, internet and electricity, interoperable payment systems, customer relationships, equality of opportunity for women, and remittances, pensions, and insurance.

As part of the Asia Finance Forum, the Fintech Boot Camp was also held on 4–5 November 2019 to provide insights and knowledge on important topics surrounding financial services and the application of technology, such as alternative credit scoring, central bank digital currency, cyber security, and blockchain.

The event brought together more than 480 policy makers, finance sector regulators, financial technology (fintech) companies, academia, and finance sector experts from 36 developing member countries of ADB who explored and discussed how digital financial technologies can help reach the still large population that remains financially underserved and excluded.

These proceedings capture the insights, experiences, and perspectives of fintech experts and provide deeper understanding on new approaches and innovative ways in bridging the gap for the underserved at the base of the pyramid.

ABBREVIATIONS

ADB	Asian Development Bank
AFIN/APIX	ASEAN Financial Innovation Network's API Exchange
AI	artificial intelligence
APEC	Asia-Pacific Economic Cooperation
API	application programming interface
ASEAN	Association of Southeast Asian Nations
BSP	Bangko Sentral ng Pilipinas
CBDC	central bank digital currency
CFI	Center for Financial Inclusion
DCEP	Digital Currency/Electronic Payment
GDP	gross domestic product
GSMA	Global System Mobile Association
ICT	information and communications technology
ID	identification
IMF	International Monetary Fund
IT	information technology
KYC	know your customer
MFS	mobile financial services
MSME	micro, small and medium enterprise
MTO	money transfer operator
NBC	National Bank of Cambodia
OECD	Organisation for Economic Co-operation and Development
OMFIF	Official Monetary and Financial Institutions Forum
P2P	peer-to-peer
PRC	People's Republic of China
SDGs	Sustainable Development Goals
SME	small and medium-sized enterprise
SMS	short messaging service
UN	United Nations
UPI	unified payment interface
US	United States
USSD	unstructured supplementary service data

ADB
3RD ASIA FINANCE FORUM
Opening Plenary
Multifunction Hall 1-3
6 November, 8:45 a.m. - 9:00 a.m.
3RD ASIA FINANCE FORUM | THE FUTURE OF INCLUSIVE FINANCE
1.7 BILLION
UNBANKED

1

2

3

4

5

THE FUTURE OF INCLUSIVE FINANCE

1.   Session 1 discussing inclusive finance
2-4.   Participants at the forum.
5.   Pre-forum activity discussing block chain for development
6.   ADB Vice-President Bambang Susantono at the opening remarks.
7-9.   Participants at the forum.

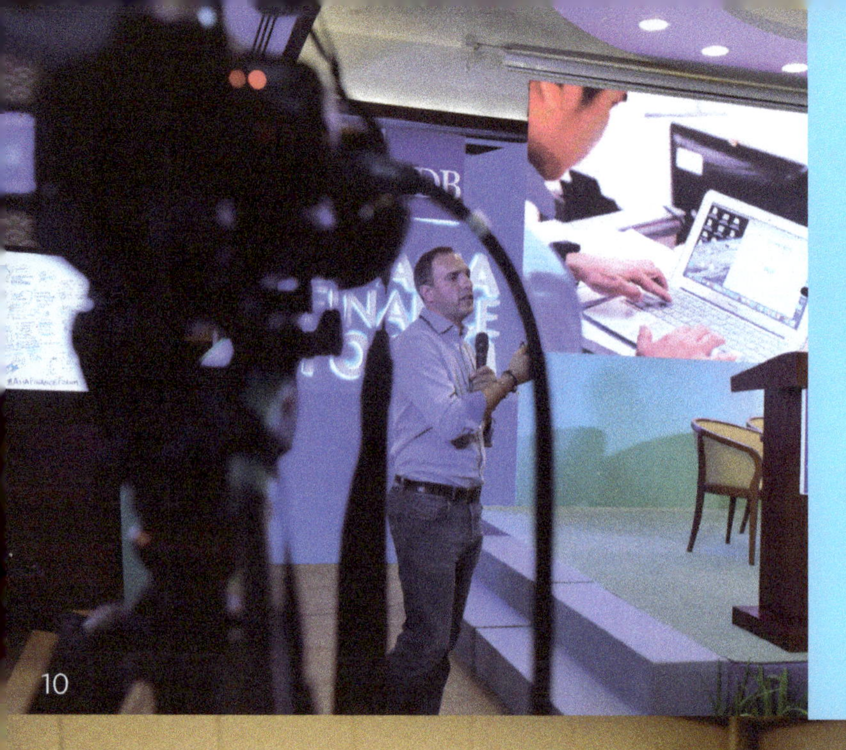

3RD ASIA FINANCE FORUM

10. Session 3 sharing stories from the field
11. Pre-forum activity discussing financial literacy and consumer protection
12. Way forward session
13. A participant using the forum's mobile app
14. ADB Vice-President Diwakar Gupta at the closing remarks
15-16. Way forward discussion
17. Digital marketplace
18. Closing of the forum by ADB organizers

10

11

12

13

3RD ASIA FINANCE FORUM | THE FUTURE OF INCLUSIVE FINANCE
6 NOVEMBER, 2019, ADB, MANILA
#AsiaFinanceForum

1.7 BILLION UNBANKED WORLD WIDE
900 MILLION IN ASIA & THE PACIFIC
ADB PILOT PROJECTS
BANGLADESH
CROP INSURANCE
PHILIPPINES
CLOUD-BASED BANKING
PNG
DIGITAL ID
BIO METRICS

NONE LEFT BEHIND & OFFLINE IN DIGITAL ECONOMY
SOUNDS GOOD!
HOW DO WE ACHIEVE IT?

DIGITALIZATION
KEYNOTE ORGANIZE
RAMA SRIDHAR MASTERCARD
ACCESS TO ICT REQUIRED but NOT SUFFICIENT

ICT — SECURITY — PAYMENTS
6 BUILDING BLOCKS
TRUST — IDENTITY — REGULATION

HOW DIGITALIZATION HELP
ACCESS TO CAPITAL
GETTING PAID ON TIME
SEAMLESSLY INTEGRATED DIGITAL PAYMENTS
SME
CASH ON DELIVERY
NEED TRUST
GET KYC RIGHT KNOW YOUR CUSTOMER
OVERCOME FEAR

INCLUSIVE
FIN TECH
NEED MORE INNOVATION
STANDARD!
COLLABORATION ACROSS REGULATORS

REMITTANCE SPEED & COST
PROTECT THE CONSUMER
START EARLY!
FINANCIAL LITERACY
+ DIGITAL LITERACY
+ CAPABILITY

VISA & I FIN. LITERACY THEATER
TEACHERS LEARN FIN. LITERACY
SOCIAL MEDIA
INFLUENCER
TRAINING MATERIAL
LOCALIZE

HANDLING INFORMATION
· DATA DRIVEN
· CREATING TRUST
CYBER SECURITY

Teachable moment
Learning by doing
Nudges
MAKE IT FUN!
CUSTOMIZE IT
RULES OF THUMB
MAKE IT SOCIAL

CHANGING BEHAVIOR
MAKING DIFFERENT DECISIONS

e-KYC
HOW DOES IT WORK IN VILLAGES
NO CONNECTIVITY
TECH SUPPORT
WHEN SOMETHING GOES WRONG, WHAT WILL HAPPEN?

BANK
ONLINE
MOBILE MONEY
NOT FOR ME
STIGMA
FINANCIAL EDUCATION NEEDED
MORE RESEARCH NEEDED

FINTECH POLICY TOOLKIT
PEOPLE DON'T BUY TECH. BUT SOLUTIONS TO PROBLEMS

DIGITALIZING BANKING PROCESS
FINCA BANK GEORGIA
MOBILE BANKING
WORK WITHOUT MOBILE CONNECTION
Mi BANK PNG
CLOUD-BASED BANKING
HI TECH HI TOUCH
ORADIAN PHILIPPINES

GRAPHIC RECORDING
www.KeisukeTaketani.com

ICT = information and communication technology, PNG = Papua New Guinea, SME = small and medium-sized enterprises, KYC = know your customer, MSME = micro, small and medium enterprises.

3RD ASIA FINANCE FORUM | THE FUTURE OF INCLUSIVE FINANCE

PRE-FORUM ACTIVITIES 4-5 NOVEMBER 2019 | MAIN FORUM 6-7 NOVEMBER 2019 ADB HEADQUARTERS, MANILA, PHILIPPINES

WEEK-AT-A-GLANCE

Time	Pre-forum Activities — 4 November, Monday	Pre-forum Activities — 5 November, Tuesday	Main Forum — 6 November, Wednesday	Main Forum — 7 November, Thursday
8:00 AM			Welcome address	
9:00 AM	Special Event: Innovations and investments for gender equality: The private sector as game changers for women's economic empowerment	Special Event: Policy Dialogue on Leveraging Technology and Innovation for Disaster Risk Management and Financing	Keynote Opening: The digital revolution: Access to Finance for All; Session 1: Inclusive Finance: Combining fintech innovation, public-private collaboration, and responsive regulation to reach the poorest; Coffee Break	Opening remarks; Keynote Opening: The fine balance between risk and innovation; Session 5: Central bank digital currencies: The good, the bad, and the ugly
10:00 AM	Coffee Break; ADB Fintech Boot camp		Session 2: Turning financial access into actual usage: The power of financial literacy	Coffee Break
11:00 AM	Digital bank / Green fintech / Blockchain 101		Session 3: Breaking barriers to widen financial access through innovation: Stories from the field	Session 6: Cybersecurity: Managing risk across the fintech ecosystem
12:00 PM	Lunch	Lunch	Special Session	
1:00 PM	ADB Fintech Boot camp	ADB Fintech Boot camp	Lunch	Lunch
2:00 PM	Central bank digital currencies / Alternative credit scoring / Blockchain for development	Guide to regulatory sandbox / Digital Identity 101 / Artificial Intelligence for financial Inclusion		Session 7a: Digital ID: The answer to speeding up know-your-customer and transactions with digital ease? / Session 7b: Suptech and regtech: Creating more transparent, tech, and data-driven approaches for supervisors and regulators / Session 7c: Fast-tracking fintech innovations: Regulator and industry sandbox
		Coffee Break	Session 4a: Going cashless: The importance of interoperable payment systems / Session 4b: Brave new lending: The promise of alternative credit scoring models and P2P lending platforms / Session 4c: Microinsurance: Expanding through education, technology, and stakeholder cooperation	
3:00 PM	Coffee Break	ADB Fintech Boot camp		Coffee Break
	ADB Fintech Boot camp	Regtech and suptech / Remittances / Alternative payment systems	Coffee Break	Session 8: Growth of new entrants: How are they disrupting traditional financial services?
4:00 PM	Cybersecurity / Responsible Digital Credit / Cryptocurrency regulation			
5:00 PM		Special Event: Innovation Challenge Pitch and Cocktail Reception	Special Event: Digital Finance Marketplace	The way forward; Closing Remarks
6:00 PM			Cocktail Reception	
7:00 PM				

#AsiaFinanceForum

PRE-FORUM ACTIVITIES

STREAM 1.1
Digital Business Building: Building a Future-Ready Bank

SPEAKERS:
Ervin Ng, Associate Partner, McKinsey
& Company

Vikram Khanna, Digital Expert, Associate
Partner, McKinsey & Company

*Digitization has introduced considerable
business uncertainty, from changing customer
expectations and disruptive technologies to
new and non-traditional competition. For
organizations to thrive, they need to tap into
the valuable and fast-growing segment of
digitally active customers. Unsurprisingly,
many incumbent banks and fintech firms
have launched greenfield, digital-only banking
businesses over the last few years to offer
digital-only propositions unencumbered
by traditional ways of delivering financial
services. But how does one succeed in
achieving scale and profitability when
introducing this new approach to banking?*

In this, the first of the boot camp events, the session
started by posing the question: What is the difference
between a traditional bank and a digital bank? The
fundamental difference should not be viewed through
the channel delivery—the app and the internet—the
difference should be viewed by the complete business
model which starts with a focus on the customer.

Early adopters of digital bank services are digitally savvy
and comfortable in accessing financial services through
the internet, a mobile phone, or ATMs, away from a
traditional bank's infrastructure. Digital banking services
offered by an incumbent or new attacker generally offer
a "hook" or "hero" product, which by operating under
a lower cost model might offer higher interest rates or
better services or some form of personalization.

But despite what a consumer may see on the surface, it
is really the end-to-end view that makes the difference.
Traditional banks have legacy technology systems and
branch infrastructure, while a pure digital bank can
build from the ground up, which provides a rethink of
technology, talent, delivery channels, and more.

The most cited difference of a digital bank is the cost
structure. A digital bank can operate with an estimated
60%–70% lower cost structure, which can provide a
completely different business model. The old ways of
working established over the years no longer apply.

There is an often-cited quote from Bill Gates that
"we need banking, but we don't need banks anymore."

So, what is the challenge? The concept of digital
banking is not new. The difficulty for banks and bankers
is the concept of change. The most successful digital
transformations at incumbent banks generally have a
commitment from top management and a conviction
to change.

Digital banks have proliferated globally, and the most cited examples in Asia are from the People's Republic of China (PRC).

Six notable elements are forcing a change in the banking industry. These include changing customer preferences, leapfrog opportunities, open regulators, infrastructure innovation, nonbank attackers, and pressure on the traditional banking model.

Changing customer preferences. Consumers in Asia are increasingly open to digital banking. Consumers who would consider opening an account with a branchless bank is 55%–80% in developed Asia and 40%–55% in emerging Asia.

Consumers using nonbank payment solutions today are 40% in developed Asia and 45% in emerging Asia. There is a proliferation of mobile payment systems and QR applications in the region such as Alipay, WeChat Pay, UPI in India, and PayNow and PayLah! in Singapore.

Consumers willing to share data to get customized offers is 23% in developed Asia and 62% in emerging Asia. Consumers are increasingly aware of their digital data that is being shared, more conscious of how companies use their data, and there is more focus on consumer consent. This is forcing not just banks, but some of the largest digital companies like Facebook, Amazon and Apple to take a stance on what it means to be ethical with data, and what is the responsible use of data.

Leapfrog technologies. The pace of innovation and change is accelerating. While it took 60 years to reach a 50% adoption rate of the telephone, it took only 5 years for social media. What does that mean for banking?

Looking at a chart that tracks smartphone penetration and financial inclusion, you can see that there are several countries on the rise in the number of smartphones that provide a great opportunity for digital banking services and financial inclusion.

Open regulators. Regulatory authorities are increasingly open to innovations in fintech. As a few examples, India launched Payment Banking licenses, Singapore has announced licensing for five new digital banks to be launched with various provisions, and many markets have launched fintech regulatory sandboxes to experiment while containing consequences of failure. Regulators are much more conscious of breaking the traditional legacy infrastructure and models that incumbents have built to encourage better services, and more efficiencies for the consumer and the market.

Infrastructure innovation. Innovations in infrastructure are underway. India is building a banking ecosystem that enables rapid innovation with four layers: a consent layer, a cashless layer with UPI, a paperless layer enabled by an electronic know your customer (KYC) process and Aadhar (India's unique ID system) and a presence-less layer.

Pressure on the traditional banking model. Nonbank digital attackers have arrived. These include WeChat Pay, Ant Financial, We Bank, Grab, PayTM and Gojek. Globally, Uber is launching its UberPay, Apple has partnered with Goldman Sachs for its Apple Card, and Revolut has launched in Singapore. As regulatory borders are opening, many of these companies are analyzing how to play in the Asia market.

A Fundamental Rethink of Banking

There is significant pressure in the banking system today in the region. Return on average equity of Asia and the Pacific banking has been drifting down toward the global average. The reason for this is twofold, being margin compression and increasing risk costs. There may be consolidation in the banking industry as banks fail to recreate themselves to survive.

Also, banks' price to book multiples have declined, reflecting investors' negative expectations. Banking has been lagging compared to valuation ratios in other industries, such as healthcare, telco and consumer industries.

All these forces are converging to drive a fundamental rethink of banking as we know it today. There are four pillars to this reinvention: (i) partnerships, (ii) technology, (iii) data and analytics, and (iv) talent. Banks need to ask themselves many questions. How can they operate like a startup? What does it mean to be digital end-to-end? How can data analytics be done from top to bottom? On Talent, 40% of all banking activities are expected to be disrupted by technology. This means that about 50% of banking staff will need to be retrained and reskilled over the next 5 years.

Banks have multiple models for how to digitize themselves. This ranges from digitizing across the whole bank, to setting up a new digital bank, or a combination of both. Banks may choose to set up a greenfield bank for several reasons including: a means to enter a new market faster, building a technology hedge against legacy infrastructure, experimenting with new technology such as analytics or artificial intelligence (AI), or defending against market challengers.

Digital Banking Archetypes

There are three main archetypes for digital banking businesses. The first archetype is a bank with a simple and user-friendly customer experience and designed for an average consumer with access to core banking products. Two examples are Jenius in Indonesia and Digibank by DBS in India.

The second archetype is a bank which focuses on a specialized product or a segment-focused play such as lending, or offering a higher deposit rate, or targeting a very specific population segment. Richart in

Taipei,China and Aditya Birla Payments Bank in India are two examples.

The third archetype is an is ecosystem-linked play by forging partnerships or working within an ecosystem with financial and non-financial products. State Bank of India's Yono and We Bank in India are examples.

Digital Banking Profitability

We see that growing a profitable digital banking business requires setting up a "virtuous cycle" of scale and customer delight. This looks at linked actions and reactions to create the virtuous cycle. The cycle starts with a better customer proposition, which allows for better pricing, which creates more word of mouth, that allows the business to scale, effecting costs go down that create more profits, that can then be invested back into the customer experience, that creates the virtuous cycle.

Launching a successful digital bank business depends significantly on scale and go-to-market strategy.
- For launching the business, the IT Capex to build is $30–$50 million and time to launch is 8-14 months, Customer Acquisition cost is $50–$150 depending on the market, and the share of IT spend in Capex is 70%–80%. The build team size is 30–100 people
- For running the business, the steady state of return on equity is 15%–30%, the accumulated losses before breakeven is about $70–$100 million, the breakeven period is 2–4 years and the run team size is 50–150.

Digital Banking: Key Lessons

- The minimum scale for a successful digital attacker bank is more than 300,000 customers, given significant investments into its digital platform, and relatively stable operating expenses.

- A step change in convenience and attractive pricing is most of the time a necessary (but not always sufficient) precondition for success.
- Profit contribution stems primarily from digital lending (consumer and small and medium-sized enterprise finance); tough to make money on deposits (given the need for high yield and competitive moves).
- Initial customer acquisition is easy; driving continued engagement or earning primary bank status requires building compelling transaction capabilities and strong marketing.

- Close linkage to an ecosystem is a major benefit, but only if internal incentives, data sharing agreements, and integration into use cases/customer journeys are fully unlocked.
- Building strong innovation capabilities (own key tech, data and analytics at the core) is essential to continuously deliver a strong proposition and stay ahead of new competitors.
- Capital availability quickly becomes a challenge, given return on equity expectations and shareholder structures—finding innovative models (e.g., loan syndication) becomes crucial to scale.

STREAM 1.2
Central Bank Digital Currency: Opportunities and Challenges for ADB Members

MODERATOR:
Adam Cotter, Director and Head of Asia, Official Monetary and Financial Institutions Forum (OMFIF)

SPEAKERS:
Philip Middleton, Deputy Chairman, OMFIF

Wijitleka Marome, Deputy Director, Financial Technology Department, Bank of Thailand

Ozzeir Khan, Director, Office of Information Systems and Technology, Asian Development Bank (ADB)

Saket Sinha, Global Vice President and Blockchain Leader for Financial Services, IBM

As paper currency declines and privately issued digital currencies emerge, policy makers are reexamining the "technology" of currency, spurred to action more recently after Facebook mooted its intention to launch "Libra," a digital currency. Central bankers are now seriously considering issuing a central bank digital currency (CBDC). In a wide-ranging discussion, workshop participants scrutinized the issue and its implications. A few highlights of each participant follow.

The financial world is at the frontier of a major upheaval in the way countries and people transact, pay, settle, and account for value, as one panel participant phrased it. This potentially revolutionary process will proceed at different paces in different regions and using different formats. But central banks and financial industry observers around the world are taking notice.

The panel discussion focused closely on a new report commissioned by IBM and put out jointly with the OMFIF—Retail CBDCs: The Next Payments Frontier. The report entailed a survey of officials from 23 central banks in advanced and emerging economies, with three of the discussants having worked on it. This included Philip Middleton and Adam Cotter of OMFIF, and Saket Sinha at IBM.

"In the next 5 years a central bank (government) somewhere in the world will probably launch a central bank digital currency," said Middleton, sharing a key finding of the report. It probably will not be a G20 country, he said, but it will be somewhere close (by) and it will be issued to meet a specific policy imperative. He added that there may well be multiple launches addressing different policy questions in different ways. "We don't think one size fits all."

However, he stressed that cryptocurrencies, ala Facebook's Libra, "are highly unlikely." This is because most central banks will guard monetary sovereignty and the idea of money as a public good provided by a central authority. As a credible, legal, stable means of exchange, and account, it almost ranks alongside the ability to provide defense and (other) social services in a country, he said. As such, he thinks that central banks will frown on private (digital) currencies.

Yet one must take notice of the major technological developments in fintech, noted Wijitleka Marome, the one central banker on the panel. "You cannot ignore Libra." She clarified that central banks need to remain acutely aware of the emerging technology and explore the beneficial applications.

She described the Bank of Thailand's own plans for a central bank digital currency, Project Inthanon, named after the country's highest peak. The Southeast Asian central bank has developed a prototype digital currency in partnership with R3 and Wipro, two blockchain-based firms. The central bank, said Marome, is working with eight commercial banks in Thailand as part of the development of the CBDC, which will decentralize interbank settlements or "real-time gross settlement." These include HSBC, Standard Chartered, Thanachart Bank, Siam Commercial Bank, Bank of Ayudhya, Krung Thai Bank, Bangkok Bank, and Kasikornbank.

The project aims to allow domestic fund transfers within the country's interbank system through CBDC tokens. The first phase of the project focused on the fundamental payment infrastructure; application of blockchain technology for other functions are being explored in the next phases. In the latest, the central bank has been collaborating with the Hong Kong Monetary Authority. The two are working on a two-tier digital token, part of a prototype for cross-border fund transfers between the two economies.

Overall, she said, the Bank of Thailand "is focusing on wholesale central bank digital currency. We want to explore the benefits of having a digital currency; as a central bank you need to understand how the technology can help."

The key challenge in dealing with a central bank issued digital currency is its integration into the basic fabric of payment infrastructure of your country said Sinha.

The technology for the applications being talked about on the panel are already there to support digital currencies. "It is not a question of technology. It is more of a policy question."

In the United States, he explained, "I can buy a Starbucks card and put my money into it and then go to the United Kingdom (UK) and buy a Starbucks coffee. That is an example of a digital currency. The same thing happens in many other countries; in India, mobile wallets have money that can be used anywhere else."

"Most of us in this room might (today) get our salary directly (into our bank accounts). We don't get cash. That's e-money and we use that money to do our transactions." The difference between a CBDC and a (private) digital currency is that the issuance of that digital currency is backed by a central bank. So instead of printing paper cash they will be issuing digital fiat. "It is the same as cash works today—it will work."

Providing a different institutional perspective on central bank digital currencies, meanwhile, Ozzeir Khan outlined a few practical applications of fintech in his own organization.

He described an ADB "sandbox" program: "the ADB sandbox program is where we provide a safe place for us to experiment with our partners and explore these technologies." His group has been discussing what use cases to experiment with and how to support them. He mentioned two areas that are getting attention: remittances for migrants and tourism.

In addition, he said, ADB is looking into how it can employ the new technologies itself for greater efficiency as an organization. "We are trying to see how we can make ADB headquarters cashless and (we are) in the middle of our own ADB wallet adventure here, a deposit facility for international employers who travel to multiple countries."

STREAM 1.3
Cybercrime: The Known Unknown Emerging Risk

SPEAKERS:
Peter Hacker, Co-Founder, Distinction.
Global

Nigel Phair, Director, University of New
South Wales Canberra Cyber Center

*As new digital technologies upend traditional
services of every description, cybersecurity
has become a major issue, one that is
almost certain to affect every individual and
company. This session looked at the major
issues.*

Peter Hacker highlighted the three key messages for the
session "Cybercrime: The Known Unknown Emerging
Risk session."

First, it is a matter of the significant probability that your
organization will be hacked.

Second, cybersecurity risk should be a fundamental
board and top management issue.

Third, cybersecurity requires very close cooperation
between the public and private sectors to tackle. Cyber
risk is truly global, highly volatile, as well as severe,
contagious, fully man-made and driven by criminal
intent. No other class of risk is like it.

Cybersecurity is a Board Responsibility

Hacker presented exhibits of a cybersecurity board
report, reminding participants that company directors
have a fiduciary duty to protect the company against
cyberattacks. Cybersecurity threats include, for
instance, distributed denial of service attack, a system
compromise, ransomware, financial theft, threat to
intellectual property, and insider threats.

A distributed denial of service attack is a temporary or
indefinite disruption of services caused by a malicious
attack. It takes advantage of the specific capacity
limits that apply to any network by flooding the target
infrastructure with traffic.

A "system compromise" is access to an organization's
computer system without knowledge or permission.
In Asia and the Pacific, depending on the business,
jurisdiction, and research considered, results have
shown that it may take up to 525 days to detect
intrusion (dwell time) from suspected cyber breaches.
This is roughly a staggering 2.5 times higher than in

North America (200 days) and close to 3 times higher than in Europe. The difference is often explained by the lack of investment priority, training, engagement, and focus by top management on cybersecurity and the absence of cybersecurity laws and data directives in many countries across Asia and the Pacific. Hacker also reminded the audience that cybercrime is an issue not just for critical infrastructure, financial services, and retail in the private sector, but also for all industries and company sizes.

In Asia, ransomware (malware that encrypts a victim's files, perpetually blocking access unless a ransom is paid) is not just about hackers asking for money but can also include destruction of systems and possibly state-sponsored activities that could be a cyberattack against a government.

Attacks on Critical Infrastructure

Looking at 2018–2019, the development illustrates industries most at risk by nation-sponsored attacks on critical infrastructure, the list (order by number of attacks) is as follows: financial services, power/energy, telecommunications/utilities, healthcare and information technology. Disruption of these services could significantly impact commerce and a country's gross domestic product.

In the past, state-sponsored attacks accounted for less than 10% of global cyberattacks, but that is now definitely changing. These types of attacks are referred to as "non-kinetic warfare." This is not a conventional war with casualties, but warfare that aims to destroy a country's logistical systems, primary data systems, or more.

Cyberattack Case Study Analysis

Hacker presented a real cyberattack case study that occurred in June 2017, with the country location changed to protect the confidentiality of the case. For this exercise, it was presented as a case of non-kinetic warfare between "perceived" state-sponsored hackers from the Russian Federation and Ukraine. The attack used ransomware in the form of a "wiper," a malicious malware, which has no specific objective other than destroying data. In this case, the attack targeted one company, which shut down email and production systems. However, the impact quickly became a global issue for this multinational company.

Hacker highlighted the four immediate steps conducted by the Case Study company when the attack was identified:
- Step 1, detect: Determine the vicious virus, the point of access, and lock computer hard drive and files.
- Step 2, contain: Minimize the impact. The company was forced to shut down its information technology systems, delivery, and management systems.
- Step 3, analyze: Determine the sites and business units impacted. In this case study, numerous company locations globally were impacted.
- Step 4, eradicate: Restoration of data (extra server), users and applications brought back in numerous locations for the company globally.

There are generally three stages throughout the incident response, which are incident triage, impact management, and business recovery. Catastrophic cyber cases can last between 9 and 24 months for full recovery. The "battle" is not won in the first 2–3 days, but in the first 3–6 months after the incident; only in a later stage do the company's business interruption, interference, and customer losses as a result of this incident become truly apparent.

Taking a final look at the case study, the company had to take its business in some countries offline for up to eight days, its supply chain was shut down for 3–5 days, and the total cost of the incident (economic and subsequent investment) was close to $100 million. The result of the incident helped strengthen the internal working relationships between IT-security, risk management, insurance and legal.

Hacker also referenced a cyber risk threat initiative addressing potential global catastrophe scenarios for governments and major sectors. The Singapore Reinsurance Association was the incubator for the initiative's launch at Singapore International Reinsurance Conference 2018 but clearly honored its independent role as a representative of the Singapore reinsurance market. The organization stayed hands-off in any of the bilateral work between Hacker and the subscribing (re)insurance partners.

The disaster scenario was quite complex as a review of a global distributed denial-of-service attack by ransomware in the form of Wiper (malware whose intention is to wipe the hard drive of the computer it infects), covering eight vectors (methods or pathways used by a hacker to access or penetrate the target system). The study also covered eight industries including government and financial services, and three incident scenarios including power outage, cloud and domain name system failure, and a combination of the three. The aim was to look at the global impact over 2–5 days for the public and private sector.

Hacker noted that in the Singapore study, an estimated 359,000 to 776,000 companies would be impacted with global impact and emphasized through a heat map illustration that cyber risk today is a global risk. Looking at the various scenarios, such an attack could mean global economic losses between $121 billion and $234 billion and global insurance losses between $27 billion and $40 billion.

The Need to Prepare for a Cyberattack

In preparing for a cyberattack, there are four areas of focus, referred to as a group incidence response matrix. These include a crisis management plan, an incident response plan and a forensics plan that identifies internal and external resources and activities, and risk transfer that could include cyber insurance or other risk management activities.

Hacker urged organizations to establish plans and conduct stress tests against the possibility of a cyberattack, and actively engage top management in these exercises, to be best prepared.

Nigel Phair presented three recent cyberattacks in Australia to illustrate the importance of the implementation of a group incidence response matrix:
- The State of Victoria experienced a ransomware attack that affected 27 hospitals, which delayed surgeries and led to the shutdown of patient records, booking and management systems. These hospitals were unprepared for such an attack, and there have been insufficient resources to handle the matter.
- LandMark White, Australia's largest independent property valuation firm experienced a data breach of over 100,000 records including property valuations, information of borrowers, lenders, homeowners and property agent data that appeared on the dark web. This caused the company reputational damage, significant loss of business, and significant share price drop.
- Through a spear phishing attack on the Australian National University to a senior staff member, hackers gained access to 19 years' worth of personal information of staff and students. The university has now spent millions upgrading its computer network.

Cybersecurity Insurance

Hacker compared cybercrime to the burglary of a house, but in the case of cybercrime the theft and damage is through virtual access with malicious intent. At a first level, cyber criminals may steal financial assets or intellectual property, interfere with revenues, or steal data. At a next level, they may steal customer data leading to privacy issues for the customer, more malicious use of personal information or network security breaches. The consequences of cybercrime at organizations can result in loss of revenue, the additional cost to remedy the cybersecurity breach, cause third-party liability claims or reputational harm or branding implications

Globally, cybersecurity insurance today is estimated at about $3.5–$4.0 billion based on premiums (including non-physical damage business interruption). It is expected to grow exponentially to about $7–$10 billion by 2025 and $15–$20 billion by 2030. The take-up of cybersecurity insurance is strongest in the US (30%), followed by Europe (5%-10%) and much smaller in Asia (3%).

Phair commented that cybersecurity insurance is still nascent in Australia. Hacker added on that companies are still understanding how this new type of insurance will pay out in the event of a cyberattack, and the insurance industry is still evolving its value proposition for this product.

Protecting the Company with IT security

Hacker reviewed four areas where a company can protect itself with IT security. The first area is open source threat intelligence (outside-in), which gathers information from public and legal data sources, as well as social media, blogs, news, and the dark web. The second area is behavior assessment, which looks at how cyber criminals around the world are operating and their target focus in terms of country, industry and data. The third area is penetration stress testing and monitoring (inside-out), such as watching traffic patterns and attacks on the system, and the last area is host based searching indicators of compromise. Typical indicators of comprise are URLs, virus signatures, IP-addresses, malware files (PDFs), etc.

Phair closed by noting that an organization's board, c-level management, compliance, legal and risk departments, and cybersecurity and insurance teams should be working together to ensure that cybersecurity is a priority. It is not good enough to just have a response plan in place. These plans need to be stress-tested (including the board) independently and regularly.

STREAM 1.4
Regulatory Sandboxes: An Enabling Environment for Financial Services Innovation

SPEAKER:
Kieran Garvey, Lead, Regulation and Policy, Cambridge Centre for Alternative Finance

A regulatory sandbox is a formal regulatory initiative to live-test new products, services, or business models on a time- and scope-limited basis. This helps to determine the appropriate regulatory treatment or status of innovative solutions to enable them to safely operate in the marketplace.

Kieran Garvey started with the context fueling the interest in sandboxes. In 2010, there were about 3,000 fintech firms, by 2017 almost 9,000, and today around 20,000 fintech firms operating globally. For regulators, this means trying to understand what these different types of firms are and whether they are doing something fundamentally new.

Technology is clearly advancing rapidly and new firms proliferating. "The telephone took 75 years to reach 50 million people, radio 38 years, the internet 4 years to reach 5,850 million, Facebook 3.5 years . . . and Angry Birds 35 days," said Garvey. And new firms entering the market are looking at traditional banking and other areas of finance and seeing entrepreneurs making lots of money and looking for new market segments. In the PRC in 2016, for example, about 9% of payments were being done by fintech firms, but by 2025 half of all payments are expected to be executed by non-bank firms, with similar trends predicted in North America, Europe, and Asia.

The first wave includes the fintech firms, 20,000 doing different activities globally and then increasingly connecting with each other. They're using different types of technology to integrate their products and services together through things like APIs (application programming interface). And banks, some seeing that they cannot compete are partnering with them. A good example is the German-based digital bank called Fidor. To make sure that all the different fintech products are also available to their customers, they are integrating with the fintech firms.

These changing dynamics are making the job of regulators and policymakers quite challenging, given that some of them may lack technological expertise of the new fintech firms or resources, staff, and capacity to look at new developments.

He defined in part a sandbox as a means to live test new products or services. Sandboxes and other kind of regulatory responses can help get to grips with and understand whether these new firms are doing anything different and where they fit. Most sandboxes will give a certain amount of time or scope and the process helps innovators to understand how they will be treated in the regulatory framework and allow the innovator to operate safely, in a regulated manner.

He said, "misconceptions abound, however I think from the industry and from regulators potentially, about what a sandbox is . . . the sandbox is not a regulatory mandate or authorization to be able to operate. It's not a free pass to operate without supervision."

The complex context of the regulatory sector into sandboxes have materialized as a possible solution. As the fintech providers go after different pieces of the financial industry by zeroing in on bits with high profit margins it "can create tensions about where (those products) fit within the traditional regulatory framework—and feed into what is possible in terms of a regulatory sandbox."

Regulators must be able to provide different services to different types of firms, he said. There's also a question of liability. "So, for example in a regulatory sandbox, if a certain type of activity is given permission, where does the liability sit if things go wrong? And in some countries, they have a lot of political support from the government who want to promote innovation or financial services development." Doing something is thus easier when there's government support behind you.

Given the complexity, regulatory sandboxes (and innovation offices) are being considered in many countries. "Of the 110 countries that we spoke to, 10% are in the process of introducing a regulatory sandbox and another 14% are considering it. There is a lot of interest in both innovation offices and regulatory sandboxes," he said.

He cautioned that the jury is still out on the effectiveness of sandboxes. Of regulators that have introduced a regulatory sandbox, almost 40% of them have said that it is too early to tell whether a positive impact has been achieved. "So, it's quite uncertain and may be quite difficult to know if a regulatory sandbox has achieved its objectives."

STREAM 1.5
Regtech and Suptech: How Digitizing Reporting and Regulatory Processes Boosts the Efficiency and Proactive Monitoring of Risk and Compliance

SPEAKER:
Kieran Garvey, Lead, Regulation and Policy, Cambridge Centre for Alternative Finance

Regtech and suptech includes any use of technology to automate regulatory compliance or oversight processes. The term was first used to describe compliance technology used by regulated firms, but its meaning has broadened to include all technology used for regulation.

Regtech and suptech is not an entirely new industry; globally, the industry generated an estimated $5 billion in 2018. It relies on key technologies to deliver its products and services, with 66% of the sector delivering its offerings through the cloud, 56% employing machine learning, and 43% using predictive data analytics. In addition, regulatory changes in the recent past have improved the operating environment for regtech firms.

These are just a few of the key findings of The Global RegTech Industry Benchmark Report, which helped center this workshop moderated by Kieran Garvey.

The Cambridge Centre for Alternative Finance has identified three broad types of regtech: to help the private sector meet its regulatory obligations, to help regulators supervise and monitor the market, and to change the regulatory process and the regulatory system and to help regulators see differences between regulation in different countries. "So, using technology to be able to gather all the regulation from different countries and to organize it into comparable frameworks automatically," said Garvey.

He noted that since the global financial crisis the number of updates and amendments to regulation have increased massively: in 2017 over 56,000 regulatory updates occurred. "The masses of change in regulation is really expensive and difficult for regulators to keep up with."

Additionally, regulated firms face a growing rise in responsibilities for senior management. "They want access to information more readily to do their jobs more effectively; given the amount of data . . . that is becoming more and more difficult to address," he said. Technology is needed to help make sense of the masses of new information.

In 2018, for a tier-one bank to build a single integrated "data lake" across all of its banks' operations would take around 10 peta bytes of data. To put that into perspective: "This is apparently the same amount of data as would have been needed to archive the "whole Way Back Machine," he noted, referring to the digital archive of the World Wide Web.

As firms face new data and increasing fines for not complying, the need for technology to help handle the vast and expanding amounts of data is thus huge and expensive.

"Globally, the differences in financial regulations between different countries in terms of compliance officers that you have to hold for legal advice, time, effort, and energy (financial service providers as well as regulators) costs around $780 billion a year," said Garvey.

Regtech and suptech covers a spectrum of different activities, he noted. He organized those by asking who is the user, is it for banks or traditional financial service providers? Is it for fintechs, regulators or policymakers? Perhaps even for helping consumers decide what product or service to access?

What are the objectives of the regtech and suptech solution in terms of where it fits in the compliance process? How does a regtech and suptech solution work? What types of technology is it using?

According to the survey Garvey referenced in his presentation, almost all the vendors surveyed (89% to 94% of firms) targeted banks as potential clients, making banks the most commonly cited clients; fintechs (cited by 68% of vendors) and law firms (cited by 61% of vendors) were second and third respectively. More than half of the firms in the survey sample (58%) considered themselves to have clients outside of both the financial services sector and advisory, consultancy, legal and regulatory industries.

Garvey loosely looked at the situations that might generate data:

> "You as an organization generate data and some of that data will come from outside your

organization." If you are in the private sector, you're going to be generating data from outside, but also internally: receiving calls, messages, emails or people speaking on the phone, and that's all generating data."

As a financial service provider, the type of thing you are doing is generating information about different transactions in relation to different services and that ultimately feeds into creating content and some of that content is going to be relevant for regulators.

"Traditionally . . . extracting the meaning from data was very manual and it took a lot of time and it took a lot of people." This has been happening for a long time. So, you have this data that needs to be processed either manually or in an automated manner by regtech solutions.

If you're a regulator you're going to have a different perspective of what data is important and why. As a firm you will map your policies and controls and they may be in relation to different areas. Similarly, with the regulator, different parts of the information might be relevant for different departments."

Through audience participation and his Cambridge Centre for Alternative Finance's survey, Garvey extensively reviewed many of the scenarios that could involve the need for regtech and suptech. He also revealed the types of clients regtech and suptech providers are serving. "Most of the regtech and suptech providers are serving the financial services sector, but there are many different regulated industries. After them, the government or the civil service, they are the top kinds of users of regtech solutions." Software, energy utilities, real estate, healthcare and so on are other areas regtech and suptech providers are serving. In addition, "we found younger and newer regtech and suptech firms were more likely to be looking for users outside of financial services."

STREAM 2.1
Accelerating Green Financing with Emerging Technology: A Practical Guide to Blockchain, Green Digital Bonds, and Country Readiness Mapping

SPEAKER:
Katherine Foster, Chief Intelligence Officer, Sustainable Digital Finance Alliance

Artificial intelligence, the Internet of Things, big data, and other emerging digital technologies are creating ripples in financial technology, inspiring considerable promise for harnessing these innovations to achieve the Sustainable Development Goals (SDGs) or meet the climate change objectives of the Paris Agreement.

If emerging financial technologies are to meet SDGs and other global objectives, this will require considerable effort to overcome a disconnect between the innovations in the fintech industry—which is striving to create applications that meet the commercial needs of its burgeoning client base—and the need for green finance. Few countries have integrated the two agendas. Instead, the body of legislation and policies needed to be mapped out is very broad and very much misaligned. So, solutions are being developed largely on two separate paths: fintech focusing on services and access on one hand and green solutions in finance on the other. This was among the messages of the workshop presentation by Ms Foster.

Regulators and policymakers are realizing, nonetheless, that fintech can be a strategic tool to help deliver on the public policy goals of the Paris Agreement and the SDGs. The fintech industry and its rapidly changing innovation ecosystem can offer solutions to unlock sustainable and green finance as well as solutions which can be deployed to that end.

Launched in 2017 at the World Economic Forum in Davos by Ant Financial Services and the United Nations (UN) Environment Programme, the Sustainable Digital Finance Alliance leverages digital technologies and innovations to enhance financing for sustainable development and financial inclusion. It would also advance green finance and investment, and insurance. It would accomplish its goals by working to better align the fintech industry and its innovations with the needs of sustainable development and policies to achieve it.

Katherine Foster hastened to note that technology is no panacea. "I'm coming (at this) from a technology agnostic and neutral standpoint." Technological innovations have produced significant unintended consequences. "We have job losses, a winner-takes-all (approach), the financial risks of social inequality, and data use and privacy issues" in addition to environmental consequences.

The information and communication technology sector has a footprint as large as the aviation sector, for example, and "this is something we need to factor in." Many early observers noted the significant energy consumption involved in the data mining of some blockchain platforms (particularly Bitcoin) and the contrast that creates with sustainability goals. We need to better explain and differentiate between "mining" and other proofs that have lighter energy consumption and build in green infrastructure in operations.

But by shaping international cooperation, promoting national ecosystems, and igniting market action, she was hopeful that fintech could be made to work for sustainable development. In her presentation, Foster therefore aimed to present the evolution of green finance and its mechanisms and initiatives that can overcome the barriers to shaping fintech innovations toward green finance.

She provided some statistical context to make clear why "we need to build new purpose into a digital financial system." On one side of the coin we have $300 trillion dollars globally managed by financial and capital markets, and $7 trillion dollars in savings, yet $12.5 trillion of savings and private capital earn negative interest rates because investors are struggling to find a safe place to store their money.

Meanwhile, challenges proliferate, with 1.7 billion adults worldwide still without even a basic bank account, one-third of the world's arable land jeopardized by land degradation, or half of its large aquifers beyond the sustainability tipping point. "There is this huge divide between the statistics that we're seeing and the transition to the low-carbon economy and supporting the Paris Agreement as well as the SDGs." Trillions in investments are needed to meet those commitments.

In other words, says Foster, "the assets are there, but the barriers to sustainable financing are many."

Some of the big issues and barriers are not necessarily about the building of the technology, but about the regulatory space.

The case of new solar energy technologies is one example. In the last 2 years, there has been a "plethora" of solar solutions, says Foster. The Kenyan solar energy company, M-Kopa, for example, has developed a proprietary patent technology platform that combines embedded GSM and mobile payments to revolutionize asset financing in emerging markets. The solar energy company manufactures and finances off-grid solar solutions.

But "what we (have seen) is a lot of solar experiments happening in regulatory spaces which wouldn't allow them either for solar to be off grid, or the notion of peer-to-peer trading, or an issue with the metrics themselves."

The issue therefore becomes "can we scale up the dialogue on inclusion of the green agenda within fintech technologies and enterprises, as well as the application of fintech for green initiatives. We need to consider both sides of the coin.

Financial technology and fintech investment are indeed on the rise. "We've seen global investment in financial technology increase . . . from over $930 million in 2008 to more than $22 billion in 2015." And by the end of 2017, global fintech funding reached over $31 billion, including general mergers, acquisitions, venture financing, and private equity buyouts.

"We need to focus in on what we mean by digital fintech. What are the actual technologies?" There's a lot of hype around the emerging technology and a lot is nascent.

Foster presented several use cases to illustrate reality on the ground and what are the actual opportunities and barriers.

She started with very well-known use cases: the Ant Forest and the G-Cash Forest in which "we see the mobilization of people in support of sustainable development and the fight against climate change, which goes to their core behavior and consumer habits."

Ant Forest, launched in 2016 Ant Financial Services Group in the PRC, allows mobile user to convert a walk or payment for public transport to be counted and converted into virtual "green energy," which they can then use to raise a virtual tree and, with sufficient virtual energy, plant a real tree. Similarly, users of the GCash Forest app in the Philippines can collect green energy by switching to green activities and reducing their carbon footprint.

In a repeated message in her presentation, Foster noted that such apps are "integrating this new technology with all of the hard-won legacy frameworks." This integration of different aspects in the approach to green finance is essential.

"Another use case, which we find really interesting, is from one of our colleagues at ING bank, which is using different technologies to provide better metrics through big data. So, artificial intelligence (AI) and mobile technology are reducing the search cost of environmental performance for the promotion of green commercial real estate loans."

This is also something being seen in different sectors, not only real estate and not just related to European or Northern Scandinavian economies. Such projects are about financing green commercial portfolios in that transition to the low-carbon economy. Green commercial loans could be repacked into green commercial mortgage-backed Securities, for example, or other bundling for sale to institutional investors through capital markets to help banks free up capacity.

However, what is important here is the labeling and monitoring of the greenness of the commercial real estate and other types of loans.

She noted that the emerging technology and fintech capacities include better metrics, such as automated green scoring, automated data for carbon from the real economy, and actual carbon market trading. "We're now addressing fungibility of carbon credits, different greenhouse gases, different carbon markets, etc. That's one of the pilots I actually did previously with the World Bank on its carbon markets framework."

We are also talking about Green Capital markets, digital green bonds, and the application of technology not only for issuance but for proof of impact reporting. We are at the stage where this can actually be integrated and simplified allowing for smaller issuances as well as time and costs savings. "This includes (Internet of Things), blockchain, and other types of fintech and we can make everyone through this a green asset owner."

She pointed out that there has been "a lot of fluff" in terms of a visio-based approach, particularly in the conflation of blockchain application and use cases, versus initial coin offerings, which were taking the opportunity to fund-raise for initiatives or products before any technology was actually built. But we are now entering a new phase of scaling up real applications and real green initiatives.

In a lengthy discussion which walked the audience through the various technologies and issues, Foster detailed numerous innovations now emerging in the green fintech space that her organization is attempting to foster (commercial, non-profit, and government led) as well as some of the barriers.

Regulators and policymakers are realizing that fintech can be a strategic tool to help deliver on the public policy goals of the Paris Climate Change Agreements and the SDGs. However, few countries have integrated the two agendas. The body of legislation and policies needed to be mapped out are very broad and very much misaligned. Likewise solutions are also being developed largely on two separate paths (fintech focusing on services and access on the one hand and green solutions and finance on the other).

The new technologies are entering a new phase in the wake of the early hype that accompanied many initiatives. Foster outlined key action areas including the need for:
* continued research and learning about digital finance potential and practices;

* awareness and multi-party engagement bringing players from finance, sustainability, fintech, and regulators closer together; and
* greater international cooperation to promote common standards, address shared risks and increase cross-border sharing for scale

And by doing the work to integrate the commercial interests of the fintech companies, impact initiatives and their innovations with the goals of green finance, these technologies can help.

STREAM 2.2
How Alternative Credit Scoring Spurs Inclusive Finance and Can Provide a More Informed Credit Assessment Model

SPEAKER:
Mohan Jayaraman, Managing Director, Innovation and Strategy, Experian Asia Pacific

Are lending institutions seeing the full picture of their consumer? Does traditional credit report data tell the full story? Most lenders today are ignoring a wealth of alternative data by relying solely on traditional credit information to make decisions. Enter "alternate credit data" such as alternative financial services, and "consumer-permissioned" data. Through these, lenders will gain a more complete view of their current and future customers and extend financial services to those that have traditionally not had access in the past.

Experian, a global data analytics and decisioning organization, is the largest global player in the field specifically related to credit bureaus. It has bureaus in 21 countries, access to more than a billion records, and 17,000 employees across 37 countries.

The company has set up Experian DataLabs in four locations with about one hundred data scientists, technologists, and industry experts focused on innovation. The team competencies include artificial intelligence, machine learning, explainable machine learning, advanced data science, non-linear modelling, new technologies, technology stack design and architecture, and new data source integration to offer top decision-making solutions.

Experian's platform provides customers a wealth of alternative data to create a credit risk profile for individuals with no formal bank credit history. It uses best-in-class analytics to leverage available information to create a customer profile that provides a 360-degree view of an individual. In the United States for example, the company launched "Boost," a service that enables users to include their utility and telecoms payments data to add to their credit file to boost their scores. Over 2 million consumers have already connected with the services and 3.1 million tradelines have been added in the bureau.

Alternate data is nonbanking data (credit-related or behavioral) that can predict an individual's ability to repay. It is collected from the "credit unincluded," people without credit history with a bank.

Growth of Alternate Data

The company estimates that out of 4.2 billion people in Asia, only about one billion have access to formal credit. Bureau coverage in Asia stands low at around 16% compared to the global average of 30%. Alternate data broadens access for this large pool of people.

Global data grew from 1.2 zettabytes to 7.9 zettabytes in 2015 and is expected to reach 44 zettabytes in 2020. Digital data is expected to increase more than 40 times from now through 2020, approximately doubling every 2 years. What is the reason that alternate data has been growing exponentially?

- The first reason is that consumer behavior has substantially changed over the past few years, resulting in an explosion of digital interfaces or digital interface points with consumers. Mobile penetration in Asia for example is 67%, with 2.7 billion unique mobile subscribers in Asia and the Pacific.
- The second change is the significant cost reduction of computing power and the cost of storage.
- The third force is open banking, a major focus area for regulators to provide access to consumer-consented data beyond credit data. Regulators have shifted their focus on economic capital only to a focus on new technology that is being used by financial service providers. They are looking at how to collect data while ensuring "consumer good," and how to maintain and protect technological infrastructure.

Open banking (that further extends to "open data") allows digital tracking of the digital footprints of these non-credit-included individuals given the high penetration of mobile phones and accelerating growth of e-wallets. Opportunity now exists to collect alternate data points (nonbank financial and non-financial data) to create a consumer profile. This addresses the issue of individuals who have no formal credit history with banks.

Alternate Data—Building Blocks

Multiple components are needed to bring alternate data models to life. Consumer consent and collaboration-based models will be the de-facto standard in the new world.

There are four basic building blocks of building alternate data models:

Data: New data in structured and unstructured form is constantly evaluated. It is estimated that formal credit scoring models generally use about 8–10 variables; alternate data credit scoring has the capacity to use more than 500 data points.

Analytic techniques: Advanced analytics and machine learning combined with a wide range of accessible data can help solve problems and improve customer insights.

Platforms: Platform capabilities are needed to build, manage, and deploy the combination of real-time and batch data capabilities.

Collaborative business models: Partnerships with telecoms, utility companies, e-commerce, and wallet payment providers can help go beyond the traditional data set.

Alternate Data Sources

In the past, credit bureaus were considered the sole source of consumer credit information and a means to reduce bad debt and alleviate systematic risk. Alternate data shifts the consumer credit data model from an "ownership" to an "access" model and demonstrates the potential strength of combining data from multiple sources.

The alternate data universe is growing and data can come from various sources:

- utility payments (electricity, gas, water),
- rental payments,
- telecoms and mobile behavior,
- e-commerce/travel data,
- wallet/payment data, and so on.

However, not all data is born equal. "Predictive value" of the alternative data varies by source and history. It is important to consider factors such as coverage, behavioral history, specificity to individual, accuracy and orthogonality, compliance with regulations—such as Europe's General Data Protection Regulation—when evaluating alternate data sources.

Data with a Gini coefficient of 40% can provide very credible insights, but data gathered in emerging markets with a 20%–40% Gini is also being viewed now as a valuable source of information. With more data about a consumer's preferences and habits, the predictive power of alternate data provides a 360-degree view of a consumer to enable the creation of a credit risk profile.

Analyzing Alternate Data with Machine Learning

The ability to use machine learning to analyze the alternate data is quite different from the static data approach of analyzing traditional credit-related data from a bank. Machine learning has a stronger predictive power for credit scoring. By using more non-standard data points it will lower the credit risk and generally achieve higher acceptance rates. Modelling with machine learning can also accommodate micro segmentations with thousands of segments and detect micropatterns on a frequently updated basis.

The use of alternate data becomes interesting and relevant to the financial inclusion agenda when combining different types of non-traditional data that is updated with frequency. By combining data points, such as bank transactions plus telecoms and utility bill transactional data, the predicted credit risk of individuals without traditional credit history becomes more reliable.

Telecoms Scores

For individuals without a bank account or financial records, telecoms data can be very useful in predicting risk level. A large set of data exists that could be accessed through telecoms subject to consumer consent and local regulations:

Prepaid/postpaid: Information of activation of subscriber identification module (SIM) card, customer tenure alongside other details mentioned in the application form, postpaid defaults, credit, churn, payment information, and mobile wallet transaction data.

Data usage: Data used, revenue generated from data, hourly usage of data, data related to value-added services, and websites browsed throughout the day.

Geo-location: Mobility from call data records, density of location, roaming transactions, as well as prominent location with attributes from census and publicly available data.

Top-up history: Top-up information, type, size and frequency of top-up alongside channel of top-up, as well as channel of bill payment, invoiced amount, payment terms, and mode of payment—bank, credit, wallet information.

Calling/short messaging service patterns: Call statistics on call duration/count, called phone numbers, towers locations, number of short messaging service (SMS) sent and received, as well as time of day calling, weekday/weekend, inactivity, calling consistency.

Demographics: Information recorded at the time of customer SIM card registration, including inferred demographic details.

Experian views telecoms data scoring for micro loans, an especially "rich data and an entry point to credit inclusion." Machine learning techniques can generate telco scores to pick up micro patterns. For example, raw call data records can be transformed into behavioral patterns to correlate with risk, ultimately providing lead generations for financing companies through these telco scores. Making use of telecoms data with machine learning can boost predictive power and increase acceptance of small and micro loans. Experian, in collaboration with the telecoms and other data providers, is at the forefront of alternative data credit scoring. It seeks to access regulatory compliant and consumer consented data, converting quality data into meaningful insights for financial institutions to consume.

Financing companies can positively gain from informed credit decision making using alternate data and machine learning techniques through a unified platform. It is estimated that these companies can increase their sales by 15% through improved credit approval rates, gain a 5% reduction in bad debt through better exposure management, and more importantly have an 80% reduction in processing time through automated decisions.

STREAM 2.3
Responsible Digital Credit

SPEAKER:
Hema Bansal, Senior Director, The Smart
Campaign, Center for Financial Inclusion
(CFI) at Accion

*Financial inclusion is increasingly driven by
fintech firms; independently or in partnership
with banks and digital financial services, they
have produced promising outcomes. Little
evidence exists, however, that these services
are being delivered responsibly, raising risks to
clients. The CFI's Smart Campaign standards
address risks to consumers, particularly from
new digital products or channels. Its newly
released digital credit standards address
a wide range of risks in accessing digital
credit, such as data privacy and security,
over-indebtedness, and lack of transparency.
These standards are meant to guide fintechs
and traditional financial service providers
undergoing digital transformation.*

The CFI is a global, independent think tank housed at
Accion International, an international nongovernment
organization headquartered in Washington D.C.

Hema Bansal reviewed the timeline of the CFI SMART
Campaign, which started in 2008 after the subprime
crisis in the United States; the Pocantico Declaration
responded to the indebtedness crisis in microfinance
and recognized client protection failures. In 2009, the
campaign launched Client Protection Principles and, in
2019, Consumer Protection Standards for digital credit
(incorporated into the Smart Certification program).

CFI works in three broad areas:
1. Creating a global coalition for consumer protection.
   CFI does this by creating a common language and
   global framework to measure and evaluate financial
   consumer protection from the industry perspective.
2. Improving market level supervision and
   engagement. CFI empowers regulators, supervisors
   and networks to understand and improve consumer
   protection nationally.
3. Leading standards development for digital financial
   service providers. CFI convened the first coalition
   of digital financial service providers to share best
   practices and lead the development of standards for
   responsible digital finance.

Two primary models exist in digital credit approaches.
The direct approach is operated by an individual, micro,
small or medium-sized enterprise with a financial
service provider or fintech firm. The indirect model
operates through a merchant acquirer or distributor.
Bansal emphasized that multiple actors need to be
considered, and the partnership model has changed the
way digital credit models are delivered.

CFI's focus on digital credit stems from several issues.
First, some jurisdictions have a gap in regulatory
oversight and overall delinquency rates tend to be
higher. In Kenya, delinquency rates are around 27%.
Globally, digital credit lending is extremely high from

62%–150%, demonstrating its perceived risk. Channels for understanding the needs of marginalized customers to create products that can be adapted to them are also lacking. Additionally, customer protection practices are generally inadequate, and users are confused or dissatisfied due to the low "touch" of digital credit services.

For CFI, seven client protection principles are the backbone of consumer protection:
1. appropriate product design and delivery
2. prevention of over-indebtedness
3. transparency
4. responsible pricing
5. fair and respectful treatment
6. privacy of client data
7. complaint handling and resolution

These standards are intended to advance practices for a variety of providers. For digital lenders—which include consumer credit and enterprise lending primarily with technology but with human touch at key points—client protection principles 1–7 would apply. For third-party partners such as data analytics firms, call centers, or external debt collectors, principles 2, 5, 6, and 7 would apply.

For mobile money operators, given limited application, principle 1 would apply. For other fintech firms and digital financial service providers, given the appropriate product design, transparency, privacy and complaints, principles 1, 3, 5, 6, and 7 would apply.

The digital credit standards introduced in 2019 include the seven client protection principles, 24 standards representing outcomes for standards, and 92 indicators representing the technical core of the requirements. Bansal briefly summarized client protection principles as they relate to digital credit. On principle 1—product design and delivery—it was noted that digital credit creates the shift from staff engagement with clients to the importance of the design of the digital user interface. Ideally, CFI would like to see all seven client protection principles imbedded in the design and delivery stage of the service. There is also an interest in having organizations offer other financial services such as savings and insurance that act as a financial safety net.

On client protection principle 2—prevention of over indebtedness—a recent survey illustrated that 62% of digital credit borrowers did so from multiple sources. Overall concern is that digital credit is seen as a fast access way to borrow that may lead to over-indebtedness. While it is critical for digital credit lending to have clarity on the borrower's repayment capacity, which would be reviewed through a payment algorithm, it is also important to have manual intervention capability to review a borrower's payment capacity. It is also important to provide the borrower with a window before being negatively reported to the credit bureau.

On client protection principle 3—transparency—digital credit information needs to be summarized with key terms and conditions in an easily readable mobile format. A local language option should be offered and an audio file made available for illiterate clients. Contracts should be simple, avoiding legal language. Continued communications are also critical throughout customer engagement, with all updates notified promptly, and a call center number available for further queries. On demand information should be available, such as payment receipts.

On client protection principle 5—fair and respectful treatment of clients—all digital credit institutions must have an institutional code of conduct (or ethics) to help employees practice fair and respectful treatment of clients with clear standards of professional conduct. Numerous stories exist of bad behavior such as postings on a customer's social media channel about overdue payments, calling at inappropriate hours, or contacting family or social media contacts.

On client protection principle 6—privacy, security and integrity of client data—policies and processes are needed that maintain confidentiality, security, and accuracy of client data, as well as data expiry periods and regular assessments to keep data current. Client consent is required when downloading an app and clients should understand how data is being used if it will be shared with a third party and how to opt out. The credit provider needs a fraud prevention system, but client education is also needed to ensure they keep their PIN safely, accept system security updates, and know what to do if their mobile phone is lost. Digital credit systems are especially prone to fraud if stolen personal profile information is used to register given rapid loan processing, making governance around privacy, security, and integrity of client data especially critical.

On client protection principle 7—mechanism for complaint resolution—Bansal explained that a complaint resolution policy should clearly define customer complaint channels with minimum performance standards. Also needed is an escalation policy, at least two contact channels provided at a minimum or no (data) cost, a means to determine the severity of the complaint, and call centers or response unit for access to relevant customer data, including transaction details and systems to monitor client interaction.

In an interactive session participants then divided into groups to identify the top risks for digital credit. Multilateral finance institutions, fintechs, financial institutions, and technical assistance providers—one group—identified issues around data privacy, collection practices, limited innovations in product design, issues of collateral, auditing of data and non-transparency as some of the key risks.

Among regulators, the Central Bank of Thailand cited information-technology and consumer protection risk among the top risks. The Bangko Sentral ng Pilipinas found that it was difficult to get fintechs to set an effective complaint resolution mechanism and enhance the financial capability of clients. OJK in Indonesia, highlighted the risks around peer-to-peer (P2P) lending and underlined the need for setting up a code of ethics with fintech associations. In Myanmar, the regulator highlighted the need for clear regulations on mobile money, especially payment and remittances. Regulators from Sri Lanka and Uzbekistan are focused on setting up complaint resolution.

To conclude, while industry recognized the risks, most providers felt that implementation of digital standards would take time and they could benefit from cross-country research projects highlighting some of the best practices as well as flagging the risks that they would need to prioritize given complex priorities.

STREAM 2.4
Digital Identity 101

SPEAKER:
David Shrier, Founder and Managing
Director, Visionary Future LLC

*The United Nations includes in Sustainable
Development Goal 16.9 the idea that more
than one billion people, currently invisible
in the eyes of government, will be able to
obtain identities by 2030. In a number of
emerging economies, banks and non-bank
financial institutions are retrenching from
offering financial services to the very poorest
customers, reversing inclusion trends, due to
the high costs of compliance requirements in
KYC, anti-money laundering, and combatting
the financing of terrorism. Next generation
digital identity may hold the key to addressing
these.*

Part of the reason nearly half of the world's population is financially under included, or excluded entirely, is because of failures in identification systems, noted Shrier, opening this session looking at prospects for digital identification (ID) to overcome this challenge.

Moreover, in the developing parts of the world—in Asia and the Pacific and Africa, the global south—economies need to create 600 million new jobs in the next 15 years just to avoid widespread famine. Four out of five new jobs are created by small and medium-sized enterprises (SMEs), which is good, but 95% of SMEs are underbanked or unbanked, again, related to failures in identity systems.

More troubling still, even when identity information is collected about people, it is unsecure and has been hacked, that is, stolen and misused. "Earlier this year 540 million user profiles and passwords and personal information were stolen from Facebook," Shrier reminded his audience. Other prominent examples are worth repeating: the billion or so biometric profiles in India's Aadhaar system, a noble effort, hacked; voter IDs in the 2016 US presidential election, hacked. "Once these identities get stolen, they get weaponized." Existing systems of ID are broken, he said, and that in part reflects the fact that identity technology has not really been updated in so many years.

Shrier described the multifaceted nature of our identities today, what he called "persona." "When we're in a work environment, we probably present ourselves a certain way. We talk a certain way. We dress a certain way when we go shopping. We probably present ourselves a little differently. When we're going out at night and so on." Existing systems do a poor job reflecting these.

So even where we have ID systems in place, they fall short. Passports with a photo and demographic information, or ID cards that now have EMV chips storing data have problems and can and have been hacked. Modern ID systems do not "do a great job adapting to how we actually think of persona."

Likewise, online, "we've repeated the sins of what we do offline." User ID and passwords are used as a way of identifying ourselves, with a few other things like machine ID or "challenge questions" and so on.

All these shortcomings in ID systems create huge problems for industry and for financial services. For example, anti-money-laundering and know-your-customer requirements have introduced huge costs into the private sector. "Banks will spend up to 20% of non-interest operating expenses just handling identity compliance . . . 95% of the time the database is generating a false positive, so banks have to hire thousands of people who manually resolve false positives from the (anti-money-laundering) system," he noted, with one major bank employing some 4,000 people to manually resolve false positives.

But there are solutions. He described a new system of identity that would combine blockchain and artificial intelligence technologies that could overcome the multiple shortcomings in our long-established ID systems.

He went into some of the basics of identity that need to be secured. These are validation—do the credentials you've presented as yours actually exist?; verification—is this accurate?; authentication—you have a valid document that has been verified with accurate information. However, is it actually you (that is you are not attempting identify fraud)? A world where robust identity systems addressed current deficiencies would feature strong "providence attributes" and include such things as self-issued personae, privacy-preserving verification, and so on.

According to Shrier, the good news is that, "there are more and more smartphones in the world. And it turns out these are really good tools for generating robust identity. You can do things like gait analysis. So how I walk the accelerometer on the phone can pick that up if it's in my pocket and that becomes a unique identifier."

Another form of biometrics, which can be useful not only with the phone but also the keyboard is biomechanical. "If I'm holding my phone in a certain manner, the gyroscope on the phone can detect the angle at which I'm holding it. The pressure sensors, the haptics on the screen can detect how fast I'm typing and how hard I'm pressing and what the delay is when my fingers move and how long they stay in one place. When I press down it's known as flight and rest that creates unique biomechanical signature believe it or not."

Likewise, how you walk around a city is a unique behavioral biometric: "95% of the time you will follow similar paths of commuting to get from home to work and then from work to the coffee shop that you go to and then which coffee shop you go to and even what you order at that coffee shop."

For purposes of identification "It's not 100%, it's 95%, but all these things are probabilistic, even facial scanning and fingerprint scanning. It's taking a guess that you're matching up with the file."

If you combine several different biometric techniques, combine facial and fingerprint and biomechanical and behavioral movement, etc., "you can get a system that's 99.99% or better," he said. And that's very difficult to forge or hack: "it's very difficult for someone to replicate holding the phone the same way."

In a detailed and complex presentation of his ideas, Shrier revealed the technical concepts involved in creating robust digital ID. He also described his own work with Visionary Future and referenced a book he has worked on exploring the creation of an "Internet of Trust Data," which would use blockchain and other emerging digital technology to achieve these goals.

STREAM 2.5
Remittances: Harnessing the $1 Trillion Remittance Market to Accelerate Access to Inclusive Finance

SPEAKERS:
Leon Isaacs, Joint-Chief Executive Officer, Developing Markets Associates Global

Jonathan Capal, Director (DMA Asia Pacific), Developing Markets Associates Global

International migrants annually send home more than an estimated $1 trillion (including informal transfers), significantly higher than overseas development assistance and foreign direct investment received by nearly all developing countries. Previously ignored or misunderstood, nations are beginning to recognize the significant benefits that remittances can bring to their economies and how they can be a catalyst for greater financial inclusion.

Key Remittances Data for Asia:

Number of migrants living and working internationally: **272 Million**

Estimated total value of international remittances sent in 2018: **$683 billion of which $526 billion was sent to developing countries**

Estimated total value of remittances to Asia in 2018: **$275 billion**

Remittances contribution to gross domestic product (GDP): **Tonga: 38.5%; Nepal: 29.9%**

Average international cost to send a $200 Remittance: **6.84%**

Average cost to send: **East Asia, 6.6%; Pacific: 6.8%; Central Asia, 7%; South Asia, 5%**

Most remittance costs in Asia are aligned to the global average and South Asia is the lowest cost region in Asia and globally. The top 10 remittance-receiving countries in Asia are dominated by India, the People's Republic of China, and the Philippines. While remittances have been growing reasonably steadily, the actual measured flows are likely to decrease this year driven in particular by challenges in the Gulf countries in terms of accepting migrants and increased barriers put up by those countries as well.

Not only are the size of remittances four times the size of international overseas development assistance, remittances are particularly reliable when other forms of financing are poor. Remittances are also quite often counter cyclical as they increase during a time of crisis.

The United States is the largest single country by volume for sending money into Asia, at 21%, but the Gulf States combined are significantly higher at around 35%.

There are different ways in which money is sent by migrants, but about 90% today is still sent as a cash-to-cash transaction. While Western Union and MoneyGram are the traditional remittance players, digital-first remittance players such as WorldRemit, Azimo, Xoom and Remitly are making headway. There is also a rise in the number of mobile wallet-to-mobile wallet transactions. In addition there are also cryptocurrency remittance services now beginning to be piloted.

Informal remittances also continue to be high in the Asia region. Note that only through household surveys or census data can the size of the informal market be estimated. Generally, these remittances are higher in countries where there is a land border with another country.

At a global level, Asia is the world's largest remittance receiving region, represented by six of the top 10 remittance receiving countries, and five of the top 10 most remittance reliant countries, based on percentage of GDP contribution.

In the Asia region, there is a mixture of global, regional and corridor specific remittance operators. There are estimated to be over one million pay-out locations in the region, about 850 million transactions annually and remittance costs paid by the users are estimated to be over $18 billion.

Overcoming Remittance Challenges through Better Data and Harnessing Technology

Costs: High costs are one remittance challenge; about $30 billion is spent on remittance fees annually around the world.

In looking at the remittances value chain, one can understand that remittances can be a complicated process. From the start it involves at least two legal jurisdictions being the sending and receiving country,

but there may be a third country if, for example, US dollars are used in the transaction or settlement process; the transaction is then governed by US regulations.

For a typical cash-to-cash transaction, there may be five to seven parties involved in the transaction from first to middle to last mile. The only way to reduce costs without earning less profit is to reduce the number of parties and "go digital". Agent costs represent about 50% of the cost in a typical cash-to-cash transaction.

The high cost of remittances is influenced by using agents, exclusivity agreements, the level of competition, compliance costs, direct and indirect costs to the remittances value chain, and the small size of some corridors. Compliance costs are large and increasing, about one half of 1% of each transaction. Most countries now require full know your customer (KYC) for each transfer rather than a risk-based approach (despite Financial Action Task Force guidance contrary to this). Also, it is difficult, for example, to create a competitive environment for corridors to countries with small populations that are often quite dependent on remittances.

Other solutions to reduce the high cost of remittances are creating greater cost transparency through financial literacy tools, as well as the introduction of financial inclusion-linked products such as direct bill payment for the remittance sender. Also important is a regulatory shift that focuses on the product offering itself rather than current regulation that is based on the historical view that remittances are a bank service and thus require more stringent "bank quality" regulations.

Informal transfers: It is estimated that as much as 50% of remittances are unrecorded funds flows. Informal transfers may be in the form of hand-carried money, sent through unregistered businesses or delivered by a bus driver. These transfers continue to be prevalent as they are generally trustworthy and inexpensive.

The top factor that customers want when they are transferring funds is trust. Given the large size of informal flows, there is benefit to studying why these transfers are successful and replicating the legal elements of these formal remittances.

Some of the other reasons that informal remittances persist are the requirement for the sender to have a legal status in the sending country, a better foreign exchange rate through parallel (black) markets, the cultural acceptance of the use of informal remittances, and that they often are more effective at reaching deep into rural areas.

Another important area is "formal remittances services that are that being settled informally." This can be best seen with the de-risking phenomenon that has increasingly made it difficult for money transfer operators (MTOs) in sending countries to open or maintain a bank account as banks view this area of business as high risk and low return. As a result, some MTOs have had to resort to informal means, such as cash being carried on a plane, to deliver funds to the receiving countries.

Governments are concerned about the lack of oversight of these informal flows which could be used for criminal activities. However, most of the large fines to banks around remittances were a result of internal malpractice or lack of systems within the banks themselves, and not the inherent risk of remittance businesses. There may also be unfair bias of remittances as a high-risk business as they are being sent to developing countries. From a consumer viewpoint, the risk remains that there simply is no consumer protection in many countries. From a policy development level, informal flows of remittances make it difficult to effect appropriate policy when the actual amount of remittances flowing into the country is not known. Lastly, countries like Bangladesh have been able to improve their international credit rating by shifting a material amount of informal flows into formal remittance flows.

Lack of accurate and meaningful data: Generally, the remittance figures that are reported today are inaccurate and understated due to the continued high volume of informal flows.

There is a tremendous opportunity for regulators to demand more data from remittance providers in the fight against money laundering and criminal activities. As an example, AUSTRAC, a regulatory body in Australia, requires that all MTOs report on each transaction such that this combined database can provide better oversight and analysis.

Also, there is much to be gained by undertaking more demand side research, especially that with a focus on gender. There are differences in the percentage of funds remitted home by gender and how the funds are managed especially for areas beyond consumption.

There is also a general issue of defining remittances. Regulators collect basic volume and value figures from the money transfer operators. Not all money transfers through operators are, however, person-to-person payments by migrant workers; some funds transfers may be for investments or donations. Being able to break this down will provide better insight.

Opportunities to Innovate All Along the Remittance Value Chain, Especially the Last Mile

Distributed ledger technology is being used by several remittance businesses, at embryonic stages, mainly in the settlement functions or compliance area.

In Asia, there are also several cryptocurrency-based remittance services. For consumers, this is only appropriate if there is a local exchange available for the receiver to convert from cryptocurrency to fiat currency. However, cryptocurrency being used for settlement between sending and receiving companies is becoming more common as it is faster than the traditional foreign exchange settlement method and often has lower margins.

We are seeing fintechs that are coming into the remittances space having pivoted from an initially different business model to focus on a specific type of remittance customer. An example is the case of Transferwise which started with a peer-to-peer foreign currency exchange model and has now moved into remittances and business-to-business payments. There are also tremendous opportunities in the regtech area for regulators.

Mobile Money is also an important and growing area. According to the Global System Mobile Association (GSMA), 78.8% of mobile money customers in the whole world are in the African region. However, there is significant fast growth in Asia, especially the South Asia region. As more of today's unbanked remittance receivers get a mobile money account, there is a great opportunity for remittances to shift away from cash pickup via an agent network to digital receipt.

Regulatory environment: To fast track mobile money in Asia, there needs be a good regulatory framework and one that allows interoperability between different payment systems, as well as large agent networks for mobile banking.

Very importantly from a remittance perspective, there needs to be a strong domestic digital payments network in place before the interplay with international remittances is considered. Research confirms that while an international remitter is likely to transfer funds once a month, mobile money receivers are more incentivized to use the account if they can spend the money received onto their wallet on a daily basis.

Building stakeholder engagement: The last area, and one of great importance is diaspora engagement. This is a key area of opportunity for governments to better understand migrants' needs and create an engagement policy that would encourage migrants to use formal remittances, undertake investments in their home country, and encourage greater usage of receivers using additional formal financial services. The key goal is to build collaboration between the remittance sender and receiver so that they can build greater financial health for their family through formal financial services education and services.

Leveraging Remittances for Financial Inclusion and Literacy

Surveys show that about 75% of remittances received are used for consumption purposes. About 15% are used for development purposes such as education and health. So only 10% remains for savings and investments.

Surveys also show that on a global basis, a large amount of funds are held in an account in the host country of the migrant worker. This begs the question of how the home country can provide investment services or other products to better harness the impact of remittances for economic growth both for the individual and the economy of the home country.

To do this, it is recommended to map the diaspora population, build trust-developing communication to both remittance senders and receivers, create incentives for home country investments, and provide training and financial education. Two examples of tools that support migrant information on remittances and other financial services include the websites, SaverAsia and Send Money Pacific.

SaverAsia was developed to assist migrants leverage remittances in Association of Southeast Asian Nations (ASEAN) and beyond. The site provides visa advice, identifies financial resources, and provides budgeting tools and other relevant information for migrants. At its core is a remittance comparison site which includes live data from an increasing number of providers. A SaverAsia app is currently under development.

Send Money Pacific is a site that has been providing remittance comparison data to migrants in Australia, New Zealand and the US for transfers to the Pacific Islands for several years. Over time, the volume of formal remittances to the Pacific Islands has increased, and the cost of remittances has decreased.

Targeted to wives whose husbands are working overseas, another example is a financial literacy program in the Philippines assisting women to learn how to manage a household budget, focus on savings accumulation, and start a small business to supplement remittance income.

Finally, the Pakistan Remittance Initiative was introduced in 2007; formal remittances received in the country that year were about $7 billion. The initiative formulated a comprehensive strategy aimed at a greater commitment of the financial sector towards remittance services and the resultant development of a remittances culture. This brought transparency to the remittance market and provided adequate consumer protection, efficiency of payment system infrastructure, and incentives for the remitters, beneficiaries, and overseas entities. Today, remittances to the country are about $21 billion per year.

Role of regulators

There are three recommended areas of focus for regulators:

Engagement: A focus by regulators to engage and develop a two-way communication with the private sector. MTOs have a tremendous amount of knowledge about the migrants who are sending money, where they are, how much they send, what they need and how to communicate with them. In some countries, working committees have been formed which have led to better outcomes on leveraging remittances for all stakeholders.

Create a level playing field: Ensure there are no exclusivity agreements (that inhibit competitive remittances business growth), allow for interoperability, have consistent regulations for both banks and other remittance players, allow different types of businesses to participate in remittance, and put in place steps to remove informal remittance flows.

Implement the global compact for migration: The Global Compact is framed in a way that is consistent with target 10.7 of the 2030 Agenda for Sustainable Development in which member states committed to cooperate internationally to facilitate safe, orderly and regular migration. Objective 20 aims to promote faster, safer and cheaper transfer of remittances and foster financial inclusion of migrants by 2030.

Specific Considerations for Asian Countries

- Implement remittance-specific regulation
- Develop national payment networks and enable remittance companies to participate
- Remove exclusivity agreements
- Integrate a focus on financial education
- Standardize and harmonize anti-money-laundering and KYC approaches
- Discourage taxes on remittances

STREAMS 3.1, 3.2, 3.3
Exploring Blockchain Concepts and the Use Case for Financial Inclusion; The Convergence of Blockchain and Regulation

SPEAKER:

David Lee, Professor, Singapore University of Social Sciences, with Malik Khan Kotadia, Co-founder and Chairman, Finnovation Labs

This double-header blockchain session focused on the technical and economic concepts of the token economy, explaining design thinking of blockchain projects. The second part of the session looked at the digital currencies Libra and Digital Currency/ Electronic Payment (DCEP), regulatory practices in the People's Republic of China (PRC) and Singapore, and the convergence of blockchain and other digital technologies.

To start things out, in the first session David Lee detailed design features of blockchain that help understanding. He outlined the most basic concepts to understanding distributed ledgers and blockchains and focused on the technical and economic concepts of the token economy and explained the incentive system of blockchain projects. The latter part of the session delved further into use cases.

The concept of a blockchain is indeed in its design: no one blockchain exists—there can eventually be millions, noted Lee.

Blockchain is a distributed digital ledger, which makes it a little more than simply a distributed database: it is a consensus of replicated, shared, and synchronized digital record of economic transactions geographically spread across multiple sites, countries, or institutions. Importantly, while a distributed ledger may not be a blockchain, a blockchain is a distributed ledger. In other words, other types of distributed ledger exist.

The cryptocurrency, Bitcoin, was an early user of blockchain technology.

The next concept Lee explained is the blockchain token, a form of economic value that is a trust carrier on a blockchain. A token can be anything that is tradable with economic value. It can be a club membership, a marriage certificate, an education certificate, a digital currency, and so on. And numerous transactions can form a token on a blockchain. Obviously, a blockchain token need not be a Bitcoin. Token ownership, meanwhile, is made clear through a "digital signature" and a pair of private and public keys. That is, "every message has got a specific identity. And that allows only one-time spending by the owner with the private key, to prevent double spending," he explained. "Who decides that this token belongs to me? This is the so-called digital signature. You need to show to people that you really own it." This is unlike email, in which numerous copies can be forwarded, for example. A digital signature is uniquely, cryptographically generated, with the help of either the public or private key, to prove the ownership and ensure correct transfer of a specific transaction.

"There's no single definition of blockchain in the market or in the literature. Everybody's trying to define what (blockchain) is, but I approach it this way so that we have a common understanding—starting from a distributor system to a distributed database, then to the chain of a blocks and associated token," said Lee.

This concept of a digital signature is very important, he noted, in that, with it, you can now start "spending digital money with each other. Even when we are offline. We can do peer-to-peer transactions, not unlike cash." He explained that this is what the new digital currency in the PRC, DCEP, is about. He elaborated further on DCEP in the second part of his three-hour presentation on blockchain.

Lee made the case for decentralized systems, highlighting the work of the late Elinor Ostrom, whose work on how people come together to preserve their collective resources, on trust and cooperation, challenged conventional wisdom, showing that common resources can be successfully managed without government regulation or privatization. "We need to be decentralized in order to increase the cost of hacking and continue to distribute trust," he said. "But that doesn't mean that you're replacing . . . a centralized authority. There will still be government. There will still be an organization that provides different forms of third-party trust."

Indeed, Ostrom's work is embodied in that of Satoshi Nakamoto, the pseudonymous author of the "bitcoin white paper" and thus the person to devise the first blockchain database and to solve the double-spending problem noted above.

Good blockchain design reduces the opportunity costs of mistrusting other parties, such as in electronic commerce and business, internet advertising, social network analysis and monetization, wireless networks, intelligent transportation, smart grids, carbon footprint optimization, and so on.

It is doing so through what are called "smart contracts." It uses tokens to incentivize untrusted parties to cooperate and thus good blockchain design reduces the cost of trust. This is defined to be the resources used in negotiation, execution, and enforcement. A token can take any form, such as nature capital, social capital, industrial capital, and so on, and allow for different designs.

It involves design thinking that will work in circumstances that will help us to entice and allow people to work together. Blockchain can solve only a few problems. But research has shown, said Lee, that by combining the technology with other innovative technologies such as the Internet of Things, artificial intelligence, and big data analytics there are use cases with societal impact.

Among the interesting uses of blockchain, Lee named several. These included SmartMesh and MeshBox; AID:Tech; and InfoCorp, CrossPay, and Sentinel Chain.

SmartMesh, a blockchain-based underlying protocol of the Internet of Things, can make off-internet communications and transactions a reality and thus hold potential for broadening services to people in underserved and remote locations. It allows blockchain to break through the internet boundary into the Internet of Things era in which all things are connected. MeshBox, a crucial element of SmartMesh, is a central node providing efficient routing, storage, and data streaming to mesh networks where smart phones and Internet of Things devices are the common nodes.

AID:Tech has used blockchain to overcome the inherent fraud in paper-based voucher systems for aid distribution. It provided 500 Syrian refugees in Lebanon with blockchain-based credit cards for buying things in a camp store, for example. With paper-based systems, fake copies of vouchers inevitably emerge. With AID:Tech cards any such attempt would immediately show up with the scanning of the QR codes on the cards.

Sentinel Chain, a product of InfoCorp, is an international platform that uses livestock as collateral through a consortium blockchain. Another InfoCorp blockchain-based service, FarmTrek, allows unbanked or underbanked farmers to use their livestock as collateral for financing within their own country by securitizing the asset and putting it on the blockchain, and thus establishing the immutability and trust inherent to blockchain. Taking that further, Sentinel Chain provides cross-border financing to the livestock-backed financing companies themselves. Livestock-backed financing companies achieve the financing by offering a portfolio of loans that are backed by livestock collateral, which is verifiable by offshore lenders. The service is near-field communication enabled, QR-code registered, and tamper proof.

Session 2: The Convergence of Blockchain and Regulation

This second session began with a brief outline of the blockchain-based digital currencies, Facebook's Libra coin and DCEP in the PRC. The session then expanded into regulation to promote blockchain as well as government as a facilitator in using blockchain as a design tool to alleviate problems that government and corporates have so far been unable to resolve. It also delved deeply into the prospects for convergence of blockchain with other emerging technologies including artificial intelligence, big data, Internet of Things, and so on.

Among digital currency, Lee presented a few details of Libra and DCEP, neither of which has been fully launched. Libra was mooted in 2019, but has raised concerns among various regulators, clouding its eventual launch. In the PRC, the DCEP launch is expected in 2020, although various geopolitical concerns are clouding the precise timing.

By way of contrast of the two pending currencies: of Facebook's 2.7 billion users, 180 million are in the company's headquarters market, the United States, leaving the vast bulk spread in markets around the world. Of the 1 billion users of similar companies in the PRC, Wechat and Alipay's, almost all are in the country.

From the white paper detailing Libra, among the motivations for the digital currency is financial inclusion. With the vast number of potential users outside of the United States, this is an advantage, said Lee. Facebook is already operating in numerous markets where many of the world's 1.7 billion unbanked or under-banked live. WeChat and Alipay are nonetheless expanding rapidly into nearby markets in Southeast Asia and elsewhere.

Meanwhile, DCEP, while centralized, retains the characteristics as a single-node blockchain without the need for consensus: it prevents double spending, manages anonymity, is immutable, secured, and transferable. It is pegged 1:1 to the renminbi, sanctioned by the People's Bank of China, and is the core satellite system with the central bank as the core and commercial institutions as satellites, thus allowing innovative business approaches in using a stable national token. It will initially be distributed to all commercial banks affiliated with the central bank, such as the Industrial and Commercial Bank of China and Agriculture Bank of China. In the second phase, DCEP will be distributed to large fintech companies such as Tencent and Alibaba to be used in WeChat Pay and Alipay, respectively.

Lee then turned the discussion to a comparison of two approaches to regulating blockchain, that of the

PRC and Singapore. "The Chinese government, as the facilitator, uses blockchain as a social policy tool," he noted in his presentation, asking "what are the risks involved in that? The Singapore government uses blockchain to grow the economy. You have really got to discern whether you want to have a very centralized setting or if you want to have certain points centralized and others decentralized to increase the cost of hacking."

Looking at regulating software projects, Lee's presentation noted the high level of commitment to the new technologies. The PRC embraces blockchain technology and its Center for Information and Industry Development has continued to publish crypto project rankings. The center is a scientific research institute directly under PRC's Ministry of Industry in Information Technology. Through it, the country has identified and ranked 506 enterprise blockchain projects; the list is a trove of insight into hundreds of enterprise blockchain projects under development in the PRC.

The city-state Singapore, however, with its 6 million people, is seeking to use the new technologies to grow its economy. It is fashioning itself as a financial hub that other countries can tap into with blockchain being used to smooth out international business frictions.

The country's initiatives include Asia's first Model AI Governance Framework released in January 2019, an international and industry-led Advisory Council on the Ethical Use of AI and Data formed in June 2018, as well as a research program on the governance of artificial intelligence (AI) and data use. These initiatives advance Singapore's vision to be a leading digital economy and "Smart Nation" through balancing business innovation and consumer trust and confidence in adopting AI. They are important principles that will guide businesses in implementing AI solutions that are human-centric, while spurring innovation in a digital economy.

Lee also looked closely at the convergence of blockchain and other technologies, with blockchain as a core technology.

In this area he compared the positions in artificial-intelligence-based financial services of the top Chinese technology giants and the big US companies. Among the former he includes Alibaba, Tencent, Ping An, and Baidu; and among the United States (US) companies, Amazon, Microsoft, Google, Apple, and Facebook. In a host of services, the Chinese companies are far more active: these include payment, insurance, personal loans, small and medium-sized enterprise (SME) loans, credit rating, money market, wealth management, crowdfunding, and currency exchange.

In this case, Alibaba et al. have clearly and actively pursued most if not all these areas while the US companies are largely limited to payments, a major missed opportunity. Ping An has made greater strides into becoming an autonomous financial ecosystem than any other company. And Chinese firms have implemented new services more quickly and jettisoned those that have failed more quickly, while US firms have suspended efforts after initial setbacks. Some 70% of blockchain patents for 2017, Lee noted, were in the PRC.

One area where there is great promise for the disruptive capacities of blockchain technologies is in commercial banking. Just like banks, blockchain services can be a store of value, payment company, credit provider, and income generator.

In general, Lee's presentation noted:
- The cloud is the foundation of AI strategy. Alibaba dominates in Asia and Amazon dominates in the US.
- Cognitive services are the foundation of AI development—voice, image, face, video, language. However, there is a "me too" and, surprisingly, a feeling that AI is already commoditized.

- SMEs and corporations can access cheap AI tools which allow them to access new forms of credit and offer new products. This is the age of the SME.
- Firms, especially in the PRC, are leapfrogging banks rapidly. They are using AI to analyze vast amounts of integrated data in order to offer new financial services to billions of unbanked people and millions of unbanked SMEs.

Within this context, the tokenization of blockchain technologies has great promise, in that it can lower the cost of trust between parties by eliminating the middleman. It encourages untrusted parties to collaborate and the convergence of technology (Web 3.0, AI, Internet of Things, and blockchain), as well as a convergence of industry. It also facilitates secured privacy protection, faster transactions, lower costs, and increases the costs of hacking.

STREAM 3.4
Artificial Intelligence for Financial Inclusion

SPEAKER:
Meri Rosich, Chief Data Officer and Head
of Data Science, Visa Consulting and
Analytics, Asia Pacific

*Digital payments are an "on-ramp" to
financial inclusion and Visa has spent the last
60 years connecting hundreds of millions of
people and organizations to a global system
that enables fast, safe, and reliable financial
transactions. In 2015, Visa committed to
payments accounts for another 500 million
people not using banking services, as part of
the World Bank's call for Universal Financial
Access by 2020. Artificial intelligence (AI)
and machine learning are embedded in Visa's
products and infrastructure and are used
to identify and prevent billions of dollars in
fraud, maintain the company's infrastructure,
and develop new value-added services.*

Financial Inclusion and Visa Initiatives

Today, 2 billion people globally are financially
underserved, some 46% of them from developing
countries and 55% women. Seventy-three percent of the
underserved are concentrated in 25 countries; 32% of
them in the People's Republic of China and India.

Visa is making a difference worldwide with financial
inclusion initiatives across many geographies. In India,
the company is working on small merchant acceptance
using an interoperable QR code-based system. The
merchant displays a code that is read by a supporting
mobile app. Also, in India, a Visa microfinance program
has issued more than 5.5 million loans issued via Visa
prepaid cards, and has provided digital and financial
literacy training for cardholders and established Visa
merchants as agents.

In the PRC, Visa has focused on rural poverty through
long-term partnerships to reach 5 million underserved
rural residents and in its targets sees 70 million Chinese
rising out of poverty by 2020.

Visa's approach to financial inclusion is to:
* provide solutions that help clients reach the
  underserved and unbanked;
* drive small merchant and agent acceptance to
  create convenience and usage;
* partner with entities that have relationships with
  unbanked and underserved populations, and the
  capacity to reach the last mile; and
* advocate for an enabling environment that
  encourages investment and innovation.

In doing so, the company has partnered with
organizations such as the Better than Cash Alliance and
the Alliance for Financial Inclusion. Key areas of focus
have been government payments, fintech partnerships,
micro and small merchants, and mobile network
operator partnerships.

Data as a Driver of Change and Growth

Data as an enabler has been called the "new oil," an analogy Meri Rosich does not agree with as oil is a scarce resource that is burned. However, she believes that data should be viewed like oil as "a driver of growth and change."

In 2006, the world's largest companies by market capitalization were the oil companies. Ten years later, in 2016, the same list was dominated by platform companies such as Apple, Alphabet, Amazon, and Facebook. This signals how data has driven the valuation of companies over the years, and this growth is further fueled by Industry 4.0 technologies.

As well, the cost of data storage has significantly decreased. Today we are enabled by scalable, massive data farms that allow data to be captured, generated, and leveraged. Interestingly, IBM reports that 90% of the world's digital data was created in the last 2 years. In 2018, 18% of internet traffic was created by Netflix and 12% by Facebook.

Rosich noted that as we talk about data and AI, the challenge is that we still do not have enough data to run deep learning models at scale. There is also the matter that when we talk about big data, we must consider the volume, variety, velocity, and veracity of the data. The variety of data refers to first and second party data, unstructured and structured data; most of what we use today is still structured data. The velocity of data is driven by the Internet of Things, such as the 500 chips located in a single car. The veracity of data considers how data is sourced, collected, and analyzed. What is interesting today, said Rosich, is how the mix of personal, transactional and behavioral data can provide blended data and new modelling techniques for financial inclusion solutions.

Visa sees three future trends that will impact the future of financial inclusion: data as a valuable growth enabler, the virtualization of money, and the concept of "markets of one."

On data as a valuable growth enabler, Visa sees change being driven by supercharged data such as the rise in Internet of Things, data alliances between the public and private sector to share data sets and break down data silos, and analytics automated with the rise of big data analytics and AI-as-a-service.

From 2020 to 2030, Visa sees data becoming a new asset class that has value and can be transacted. Also, data that was previously gated and siloed will be stored on platforms that enable easy sharing. Last, data that is collected throughout the customer journey in real-time will shift from a one-way touchpoint to two-way feedback loops to tailor the experience and product offerings to customer behaviors and preferences. On the virtualization of money, the relevance of cash is decreasing and there are a growing number of ways to use biometrics to assign identity for financial transactions.

In Sweden, a start-up is already using a near-field communication chip embedded under the skin for payment transactions—this is no longer fiction, it is reality.

Visa sees the virtualization of money being driven by democratized access through better connectivity and access to technology even for marginalized groups. Decentralized trust, as consumer concerns around data privacy and security increase, will be addressed by the new technology and trusted data sharing frameworks. Agile living in the rise of the access economy will drive demand for automated payments and fast money.

From 2020 to 2030, physical form factors of payment like cards or cash will disappear; any form of biometrics, even a tattoo, could create a point of sale opportunity. A payment will become more natural, seamless, and transparent. Algorithms will determine product recommendations and experiences, with trusted consent by consumers. Shifting from automated payments, small ticket purchases will happen automatically in the background. Consumers will only be asked to authorize the transaction when it is a big-ticket purchase.

Markets of one is a shift from personalization to hyper-individualism. Driving this shift is "flexi identities" and the numerous ways that we can identify ourselves today. Conscious consumption is thinking beyond price and making the right choices, and modular processes such as the adoption of new technology (such as 3D printing) that will reduce the costs of customized design and production.

From 2020 to 2030, Visa sees a shift of consumers trusting choices to algorithms that are able to make increasingly more accurate decisions. A shift of corporate social responsibility, not just for public relations but for resilience, and moving from mass customization to individual customization by sending the right message at the right time, and "telling me what I need and what is best for me."

In her talk, Rosich made numerous other points on how AI is impacting our lives today, how companies are using AI, and the importance of AI governance models:

- AI is defined as the theory and development of computer systems that perform and act like humans. If you have Google Home, Alexa or Siri, you are already engaged with AI.
- There has been an evolution from AI to machine learning to deep learning. Deep learning is a system of statistical and mathematical methodologies that can find solutions to problems at very high speed.

- A lot of companies are investing in AI teams and research, especially companies with a lot of structured data to find solutions to problems that was not possible before.
- AI can be used for policy making, such as using satellite images to inform agriculture. Another example is using deep learning to track automobile traffic for the development of smart cites. AI can even be employed in tracking keywords in company investor meetings to track trends.
- An example of deep learning at Visa is "Travel Predict," which helps card issuers predict travel in the coming 3 months based on transactional data that can potentially predict the city of travel.
- Another element of AI modelling is understanding the probability and severity of harm, which will determine AI governance models to monitor and prevent harm.

In her talk, Rosich noted that financial regulators will want to set standards on how AI models operate, are trained, and evaluated within the financial services industry.

She also spoke at length about the element of trust. Some companies today are losing the public's faith based on how they have chosen to monetize their consumers' data. Companies today need to establish their data culture; the standards should be set high. Consumers need to be empowered and maintain privacy, while organizations create value, maintain transparency, and are accountable.

STREAM 3.5
Mobile Money Embracing Payments as a Platform in Asia

SPEAKER:

Ruan Swanepoel, Head of Mobile Money, Global System Mobile Association (GSMA)

After a decade of growth, mobile money continues to provide innovative services that are having a profound commercial and social impact in emerging markets. The Asian landscape is evolving fast, however increased competition and strong growth in smartphone penetration are propelling evolution towards a platform-based approach, connecting consumers with third-party services across diverse industries. This session explored recent innovations and emerging trends from Asia. What are the key regulatory challenges in the region? What are the enablers to accelerate growth?

Today around 5 billion people are connected through mobile and 3.8 billion of those are in low- and middle-income countries. This demonstrates the power of mobile to connect people and transform lives.

Mobile money can drive financial inclusion to the most marginalized populations by building a full payments ecosystem. One of its most important factors is that it is a pre-funded model. This money must be secured in a trust fund at a bank, so there is little risk consumers will lose their money, and its basic functionality is as a store of value, in an e-wallet so the customer can send and receive money. It is not a savings account; no interest is paid.

Compared to a bank account, there is typically a low know your customer (KYC) requirement, which means that it doesn't have the same requirements as opening a bank account. However, this also means limits on the amount of money stored, typically $1,000–$5,000 on average in most markets. There are also restrictions on velocity—the amount of money that you can cash in and cash out and transfer daily.

Agents perform cash in and cash out; at no stage does the money leave the ecosystem. Mobile money is a closed-loop system. It is just the e-value flowing from the agent's wallet to the customers wallet in exchange for physical cash, and the reverse for exchange of a physical cash deposit. There is also peer-to-peer transfer, which is effectively a transfer of e-value between two customers of the same platform.

Mobile Money in Tanzania

In 2008, this story was all about trust. Less than 5% of the population had bank accounts, and moving money (physical cash) across the country was handled by an agent on a local bus, which cost 10% of the fund transfer amount and took 2–3 days. When buses had accidents on bad roads the cash was lost.

By 2017, the introduction of mobile money in Tanzania had transformed access to financial services. Sixty percent of the population had a mobile money or bank account and mobile money could be accessed through a cash-in/cash-out network of more than 50,000 agents, compared to a physical bank network of only 300 branches. Mobile money customers could also send and receive funds instantly and pay bills to more than 100 organizations for electricity, water, or buying airtime.

Importantly, funds held in an e-money wallet are separate from those for pre-paid mobile airtime that is purchased and branded differently. While a consumer can use money from the e-wallet to purchase airtime, funds held in an airtime account (considered as goods and services) are not transferable back to the e-wallet.

In 2015, Tanzania was also one of the first countries to facilitate interoperability such that the mobile money operators connected to each other as well as the banks. These relationships were established through bilateral arrangements with no central switch.

Keeping the mobile money model of pre-funding intact, the banks maintain a pre-funded account with the mobile money operator so that consumer payments between a bank account and a mobile money account could be processed instantly. Also, banks provided payroll services for corporate customers and distributed these salary payments to mobile money accounts.

Across many mobile money operators, merchant payments are developing, as are credit and insurance.

Role of Agents

Agents are core to a mobile money operator business model, mainly "mom and pop" shops. In the case of many African countries, the mobile money agent networks created an infrastructure and access to banking that did not exist in the countries.

At the start of an agent network, the mobile money operator will need to pre-fund the agents to create liquidity in the mobile money ecosystem. Over time, each agent will decide how much funds are kept in its mobile money account, which will be used for cash-in/ cash-out transactions, earning a commission on each transaction.

Each agent operates its own private business and would determine which goods and services are represented at the shop. Mobile money operators have an onboarding program for agents to train them on all aspects of the mobile money business such as anti-money-laundering training, how to register a new customer, financial literacy training, and more.

Agent models and commission structures vary across operators and countries. Generally, non-exclusivity in the agent model is considered best practice. While commission rates and the fee structure for agents also varies, a tier-based fee structure based on sales value is considered the most commercially-driven model, however due to the complexity of the tier-based fee structure for agents it is sometimes substituted with a flat fee structure. As these "mom and pop" shopkeepers also earn commission from the fast-moving consumer goods companies such as Unilever and Proctor & Gamble, commissions paid and liquidity required by mobile money operators need to be aligned with the shopkeepers' capacity to provide a variety of goods and services at their shop.

Mobile Money Launch: Regional Differences

The launch of mobile money services in Africa and Asia started at different times and evolved with different types of players. In Africa, mobile money launched in environments with low smartphone penetration, scarce e-commerce activities, and the need to operate offline. Agent networks have been built across countries via "mom and pop" shops creating nationwide banking infrastructure from scratch, connecting their customers through feature (unstructured supplementary service data, USSD) phones, and more recently offering services through smartphone apps. Promoting airtime was a primary service offered by mobile operators, with many bonuses for customers to buy using the e-wallet. Airtime top-up purchased through the agent was also cost effective for the mobile operator compared to other sales channels.

In Asia, while there are mobile money operators, there are also non-mobile phone operators that have created "super apps" providing e-wallets and financial services from their existing customer bases. In the People's Republic of China, WeChat started as a social network and over time developed its successful WeChat Pay service. Transportation companies such as Gojek and Uber have also created e-wallets and offer financial services across customer bases and driver networks.

To clarify, many e-wallets have developed in Asia that are not considered "mobile money," such as Alipay and WeChat Pay, as they are directly linked to bank accounts. Several banks have also developed e-wallets that provide peer-to-peer (P2P) payments and merchant payments, but again are not considered "mobile money." Mobile money is defined as an account not directly linked to a bank account and residing on a mobile platform.

Global Data

According to GSMA, around 866 million accounts existed at the end of 2018, and an estimated one billion by the end of 2019. Now, 272 mobile money deployments exist across 90 countries, 62 of them with more than one million accounts. The new GSMA report will be available February 2020.

The industry is now processing over $1.3 billion per day with digital transactions growing at more than twice the

rate of cash-in and cash-out. A typical mobile money customer transfers $206 per month. And notably, digital transactions are growing at more than twice the rate of cash-in and cash-out, good indication that a lot of use cases exist to keep money in the ecosystem. The agent network is a costly part of the business, and the increase in digital transactions versus cash-in/cash-out lowers cost for customers and mobile money operators alike.

Four key trends in are under way in mobile money:
- Enhanced customer experience.
- Diversification of the financial services ecosystem. Five years ago, mobile money was only considered a mobile operator play, but today many different flavors of mobile money are offered by several different types of industries and sector players.
- Expansion of the mobile money value proposition.
- Increasingly complex regulation.

Asia Trends

In Asia, registered mobile money customers have grown to over 382 million and activity rates have increased to 31% as of December 2018. It is the fastest growing region globally.
- While East Asia and the Pacific has seen several new deployments, customer growth has been driven by existing deployments. From December 2014 to December 2018, mobile money deployments increased in South Asia from 38 to 40 and in East Asia and the Pacific from 29 to 41. This is a good indication that mobile money is starting to scale, and use cases are addressing customer needs.
- In fact, East Asia and the Pacific experienced the highest year-on-year account growth at 38%, and now represents 11% of registered accounts globally.
- In past years, the share of the combined adult population in Asia with a mobile money account increased rapidly. From 2013 to 2018, South Asia had a compound annual growth rate of 63% and

East Asia and the Pacific 44%; 22% of adults in South Asia have a mobile money account, and 19% of adults in East Asia and the Pacific have a mobile money account.

- Transaction values in Asia have grown exponentially, passing $12 billion per month as of December 2018, a 245% growth rate since 2014.
- The different transactions on a mobile money platform include P2P transfers, bill payments, bulk payments, international remittances, merchant payments and airtime top ups. In Southeast Asia, P2P transactions still represent the bulk of values transacted. In South Asia, bill payments represent a higher proportion of transactions than average.
- During 2018, international remittances and merchant payments were the two fastest growing use cases in Asia.
- During 2018, Asia also saw the highest drop in transactions processed through USSD channels. Smartphone adoption was the main driving force. In 2018, 60% of the mobile money transactions in Asia were done via smartphones and is expected to increase to 82% in 2025.
- While many mobile money deployments globally are now reporting healthy margins, in Asia margins are lower or negative.
- International remittances are a key driver of mobile money globally, especially in Asia. There are many partnerships between money transfer operators and banks (and a growing number of mobile money accounts) on the sending side to mobile money accounts on the receiving side. This is creating a shift from cash pick up to receipt into a mobile money account and decreasing the cost of international remittances. Remittances is an area where regulators can play an important role to support and incentivize transfers to mobile money accounts.

However, while many mobile money deployments globally are now reporting healthy margins, in Asia the margins are lower or negative. This is mainly due to the competition in the markets in Asia. A lot of venture capital money is going into payments, and many young start-ups have cashback models. This is unfortunate because many of these startups cannot really scale, they run negative margin business for 1 to 2 years and then exit the industry. Unfortunately, remaining players are then not able to monetize the business.

Other players in Asia that make their money on ride-hailing or other services have already scaled up, such as Alipay, WeChat Pay, GoJek, and Grab. Payments are not really a revenue driver or a business driver for them so they can offer payments for free; they can monetize their business somewhere else. To survive in the mobile money business, companies need to scale, and these companies have effectively done so through their existing large customer bases.

While many mobile operators moved into e-wallets and payment services successfully, they have not been as successful in social platforms or non-transactional financial services. In 2018, many non-financial players invested in mobile-based payment businesses and are directly competing with the mobile money players.

Future Focus on Mobile Money in Asia

In a GSMA survey, it was concluded that ecosystem development, bank integration, and increasing rural penetration are the top priorities for the mobile money industry in Asia.

In the 2010s, African mobile money operators started integrating with banks, and found that this was a cost-effective means to drive revenue growth.

Mobile operators and subsequently mobile money's rural presence has differentiated them from other payment platforms with banks and fintechs, which have focused more on the urban, semi-urban, and peri-urban digital customers.

While the number of unregistered customers transacting over the counter has declined, opportunity remains to migrate more customers to e-wallets. The benefit is that transactions not over the counter are significantly higher in terms of revenue per customer, because these customers start using other services. The industry is therefore trying to get people to use mobile e-wallets.

Asia's mobile money deployments can also expand the number of integrations within the ecosystem. Growth with online merchants is healthy, in line with Asia's growth in e-commerce adoption and smartphone penetration. Integration with banks is also healthy; the best performing mobile money providers have close to 30% of their active customer base receiving salaries through mobile money.

The area where mobile money operators need to focus globally is integration with (physical) merchants. The number of merchants today is too low; this is an area that needs significant focus, as merchant payments will significantly reduce the cost of mobile money services and stop people going back to cash. Today, industry statistics still show that 75% of mobile money revenue is derived from (expensive) cash-out fees. These revenues generated from cash-out mean that operators still carry the high cost of cash-out, rather than the ideal mobile money operating model that keeps e-money in the ecosystem.

Close to 80% of providers responding to GSMA's global adoption survey reported that most of their revenues were driven by customer fees. Transitioning away from a revenue model heavily reliant on customer fees to a diversified revenue model stemming from businesses and governments is crucial to ensuring that the mobile

money industry can continue to serve customers sustainably and ensure the underserved are not left behind.

In 2018, more mobile money providers shifted focus to expanding value to adjacent services, including enterprise solutions, credit, and savings.

Mobile Money Regulatory Focus

Data Regulation: Many governments want sovereignty of data rather than allowing cloud-based solutions in other jurisdictions. This hinders companies wanting to scale, creates higher cost factors, and ultimately these costs will be passed to the consumer.

Taxes on Mobile Money: Many governments view the large value flows of mobile money as a taxation opportunity to assist with government deficits. Taxation on mobile money would harm digital financial inclusion as taxation would incentivize people to stay with cash.

Many countries have national financial inclusion strategies that are expected to bring more collaboration between public and private sectors to achieve this common goal. The GSMA has an online Regulatory Country Index that scores 80 data points to demonstrate enabling regulations for mobile money for financial services regulators and policy makers.

National identification (ID) is another unresolved issue in many countries and is critical for electronic KYC. Around one billion people globally have no ID. Digital ID is a key area of focus to ensure that everyone has access to telecommunication, internet, and digital financial services.

Innovations and Investments for Gender Equality: The Private Sector as Gamechangers for Women's Economic Empowerment

MODERATOR:
Amanda Satterly, Senior Social Development Specialist (Gender and Development), Private Sector Operations Department, Asian Development Bank (ADB)

OPENING REMARKS:
Michael Barrow, Director General, Private Sector Operations Department, ADB

SPEAKERS:
Alison Eskesen, Vice President (Asia Pacific), Mastercard Center for Inclusive Growth

James Soukamneuth, Director, Impact Investing Partnership Director, Investing in Women

Pia Roman Tayag, Managing Director, Center for Learning and Inclusion Advocacy, Bangko Sentral ng Pilipinas (BSP)

This panel session brings together leaders from across the public and private sector to share their successes and learnings from driving greater economic inclusion of women through innovation, technology, and gender lens investing.

Michael Barrow, Director General, Private Sector Operations Department, ADB welcomed everyone to this session which launched the ADB's third Asia Finance Forum. He thanked everyone for joining the opening session on how the private sector can be a catalyst and game changer for women's economic empowerment.

ADB Comments on Women and Finance: Gaps and Challenges

There are important gender challenges in both finance and innovation that mean women risk being left behind by these digital transformations in the finance sector.

For women in business, the Asia and the Pacific region has the largest global financing gap for small and medium-sized enterprises. Fifty-nine percent, or roughly $1.2 trillion, of the gap is attributed to credit constraints faced by women-led businesses. While fintech and other digital technologies hold great promise to reach the last mile for financial inclusion, women in the Asia Pacific region are still less likely to own a mobile phone, or to use the internet than men. Indeed, in South Asia, women are 38% less likely to own a mobile than men.

In the corporate sector across the region as well as globally, women remain a minority. Although three countries in the region are among the top 10 economies worldwide with women in senior management positions—Philippines (39%), Thailand (37%) and Indonesia (36%)—the average hovers around 15%, falling as low as 7% in Japan for example.

Women's representation on corporate boards is even lower. On average across Asia, women represent only 8% of corporate board seats. These are not only bad indicators of diversity but makes for a poor business case. A McKinsey study found that companies with the highest percentage of women in executive committees delivered better performance than those with all-male executives—the former exceeded the latter by 41% in return on equity, and by 56% in operating results. A study of 2,360 companies found that those with one or more female board members delivered higher average returns on equity, and better average growth.

ADB and Strategy 2030

Investing in women is smart economics: smart for business, smart for innovation, and smart for inclusive growth. It is for these reasons that ADB is stepping up its commitment to accelerating progress on gender equality in our operations. Last year, ADB adopted Strategy 2030, which includes an increased target of 75% of all our operations, promoting gender equality by 2030.

For the first time, these corporate targets also include private sector operations.

At present, these appear daunting since less than half of private sector transactions currently include pro-active gender targets.

The majority of ADB's private sector gender-mainstreamed projects to date have been in the finance and agricultural sectors. We are increasing our efforts to mainstream gender into our projects in the health, education and infrastructure portfolios. The targets may be daunting, but ADB is well on its journey to take advantage of new opportunities to make them achievable.

ADB Private Sector Operations Department Investments in Gender Equality

Barrow shared recent examples of how ADB is already investing in women through its private sector operations:

Gender lens investing: ADB is working with private equity investors to develop an easy to use Investee Gender Scorecard which enables the investor to quickly evaluate whether investing in a potential investee would improve gender inclusiveness in that industry. The Scorecard does this by comparing the potential investees' gender inclusiveness in terms of ownership, management, staffing, customers and suppliers with respect to its industry's averages. This enables the investor to determine to what extent its investment will result in the improvement, or hinderance, of gender equality within that industry.

Gender equal workplaces: ADB seeks to influence all of its partner clients to increase the gender inclusivity of their own workplaces by firstly ensuring that the fundamentals are in place: equal pay for equal work, a properly implemented anti-sexual harassment policy, sex-disaggregated sanitation facilities etc. In addition, we also look for opportunities for the client to improve their gender inclusiveness at all levels of staffing and in all occupational spheres e.g., through mentorship, internship or scholarship programs.

ADB Trade Finance Program's (TFP) gender initiative: In 2016, ADB's Trade Finance Program launched the first phase of its gender initiative to promote more women in banking. The initiative consisted of a gender audit of several partner banks who volunteered to assess their institutional gender equality and to provide concrete recommendations to attract, retain, and promote more women in banking.

Nineteen banks from 8 countries participated in the study for phase one and implemented 25 recommendations. This year, a second phase of the initiative was launched to expand the number of banks participating and to provide additional support for implementation of these recommendations. The TFP holds an annual gender award for the best performing bank on gender equality. This year's winner was Habib Bank from Pakistan.

We-Fi: First gender bond in the Pacific: This year, through the support of the Women's Entrepreneurship Finance Initiative (We-Fi), ADB has been working in the Pacific to provide vital finance and capacity development programs for female-owned SMEs. In Fiji, ADB is working with a local bank to launch the Pacific's first gender bond.

The bond proceeds will be used by the local bank to finance a portfolio of female-owned SMEs. This is an exciting use of blended finance, and ADB welcomes the opportunity to be able to innovate with the first blended finance grant focusing on gender equality. In addition, the We-Fi grant will be used to support a client in Papua New Guinea to develop digital technologies to better outreach to and serve their female SME clients.

Barrow closed his opening remarks by reiterating that ADB and the Private Sector Operations Team is working in many ways to increase women's inclusion in finance and in overall economic activities.

He commented that he has personally been encouraged by the "sea change" that he has seen by the commitment of ADB staff on this important gender topic, but also by ADB's clients—from SMEs to international corporates—and how they are embracing how women's economic empowerment can be an important business driver.

Panel Session

Moderator: *What is your initial response to the topic of "Innovations and investments for gender equality: the private sector as gamechangers for women's economic empowerment"?*

James Soukamneuth, Investing in Women: Based in the Philippines and supporting Indonesia, Viet Nam and Myanmar, Investing in Women is a $100 million initiative of the Australian government that started in 2016, and will continue through 2023 with the aim to support women's economic empowerment through grants and collaboration with the private sector.

The program defines women's economic empowerment as access to control over and ownership of productive assets. Investing in Women sets up large coalitions working with the private sector to promote workplace gender equality. The largest pillar serves as a "fund of funds" providing blended finance grants to impact investors to mobilize capital for female-owned and female-led SMEs. Moving forward the program aims to partner with more Asian impact investors.

Pia Roman Tayag, BSP: The private sector is the driver to expand the reach of the financial system and ensure gender equality. As the regulator and policy maker, BSP is the enabler and partner to the private sector.

At BSP our approach is to first gather evidence and understand each situation. BSP launched its National Financial Inclusion Strategy in 2015. We use evidence-based policy making to steer our course of action for Financial Inclusion and will do the same to steer the gender balance to achieve inclusive finance to fill the gaps and overcome any barriers.

The Philippines is in a unique situation as it is one of the few countries that has a 'reverse gender gap'; female are two times more likely to have an account versus men. With this evidence, BSP probably "rested on our laurels" for too long and looked at the topic of financial inclusion without a gender lens as there appeared to be no urgency to do so.

However, looking more closely at the data, it was discovered that simply looking at the numbers of how many women had an "account" was simply a "tick box" exercise. The data showed that while women were more likely to have an 'account', comparatively, men were more likely to have accounts at a bank and were more likely to have electronic money accounts.

When we looked more closely at the scope of financial services, we saw that men were also more likely to have investments. We realized that there is much more to do to make sure that that the inclusion is meaningful and effective for everyone to ensure gender equality.

With technology, it is more cost effective today for BSP and our supervised institutions to collect sex-aggregated data that will allow us to look more deeply at the gender topic. In the Philippines, more than half of the small businesses are led by women, and yet they have problems to scale and keep the business afloat. There may be a scope of financial services that female-led SMEs need that requires further investigation.

In BSP's role as an enabler, partner, convener, we also have the ability to generate data to share with the private sector. We will look more closely at the gender issue, and particularly on the link to inclusive growth with a focus on agriculture and micro, small and medium enterprises (MSMEs).

Alison Eskesen, Mastercard Center for Inclusive Growth: In responding to the question if private sector should have a role in women's economic empowerment, the answer is emphatically "yes"! The private sector has the "know how" on how to accelerate and to scale because this is how the private sector makes its financial profit.

The Mastercard Center for Inclusive Growth is a philanthropic organization and our aim is work with the private sector to inject international development best practices. While the private sector has an incredibly important role to play, they don't necessarily have the expertise or focus on how to include women and think about "additionality." Additionality in this case asks the question, "what is lost by not thinking about women"?

There is an incredible role for governments, private sector, civil society and international development organizations to play to bring together the expertise to deliver products

that are meaningful, useful, and secure and can be a driver for women's economic empowerment. The question is "how" to achieve meaningful social impact that drives growth that is inclusive.

The most recent Findex report shows that financial inclusion has accelerated dramatically, but this was mostly driven by India and the People's Republic of China. Digging deeper into the numbers, and while account ownership is on the rise, there is a low percentage of actual usage of financial services. For most people in the world, having a bank account is simply a 'symbol of prosperity' affording the ability to save money, plan for the future, and have a safety net.

Mastercard committed with the World Bank to financially include 500 million individuals and are on the cusp of achieving that goal. However, Mastercard sees financial inclusion—having an account—as only a "first step." The end goal is not financial inclusion but should be "financial security."

Moderator: We hear a lot about gender lens investing, but it remains a mysterious term for many. What is the definition of gender lens investing, and what are concrete examples?

Soukamneuth, Investing in Women: Gender lens investing is aligned with impact investing. There needs to be some measurability and some intentionality to create gender outcomes. This is like impact investing, which is about social and environmental outcomes. This is the starting point to understand gender lens investing.

There must be a strategy of accountability and targets to achieve greater results with this type of financing—Impact and Gender Lens investing. These investments also may take greater risks to improve the impact side, which could create a trade-off with financial returns.

On gender lens investing there are three categories of gender outcomes: 1) to support female entrepreneurs,

2) to promote workplace gender equality, and 3) to improve the lives of women and girls through products and services that are provided in the marketplace. This is the 'what' of Gender Lens investing.

But in addition to the "what" of Gender Lens investing, the process is also important. To give an example, at the beginning of the program, we had a mandate to increase investments in female-led SMEs. We asked our impact investors and fund managers partners: How many women are on your investment team? How many women are on the Board of the companies that you invest in? How many women are impacted throughout your portfolio? They did not know or could not track these fundamental numbers.

We had to "dial it back" as we realized that it was not just about pointing capital at gender work, but our partners needed organizational change. We worked with impact investors to create organizational change.

The investment, financial services and banking industry is a very male-dominated industry. We realized it is difficult to introduce gender work outcomes in an environment that itself does not have a gender inclusive work environment. Gender Lens investing is not only about 'what' you invest in, it is also important to look at the process.

For investing in women, there are 5 categories of Gender Lens investing as a process:
1. How is gender a factor of analysis in the investment from deal sourcing to post-investment monitoring?
2. We expect partners to promote and communicate their own strategy that is gender inclusive, both internally and externally through their website and other public domains.
3. Corporate culture is important. We provide advisors to assist with organizations that are male dominated and need support to create gender lens action plans for their own organizations.

4. Data, metrics and accountability are essential to get good results. There must be measurability, accountability, and a point person.
5. Putting in place policies is essential, but there must be the appropriate human and financial resources in the gender lens investment process to achieve an effective gender outcome. We provide gender lens investing experts to our partners.

Moderator: *How are you using evidence-based research to influence policy with private sector?*

Roman Tayag, BSP: Evidence-based research is very important, but at the same time, you need to ask the right questions. We have learned that only asking about basic data such as account ownership is insufficient.

We have recently issued regulations around agent banking as well as a focus on the growth of electronic payments and are looking at how to better understand the gender question. This is a process and a journey to ask the right questions.

BSP acts as a convener. The commencement of the National Financial Inclusion Strategy has rallied support from the private sector to bring forward solutions. In the same way, BSP can act as a convener to ensure that women's economic empowerment is achieved through these activities.

Moderator: *Do you have an example of how technology and innovation can create scale in a business idea that can benefit women business owners?*

Eskesen, Mastercard: Mastercard has a global partnership with Unilever. Together we solved a business challenge for Unilever whilst creating access to credit for micro-entrepreneurs, many of whom are women.

We discovered that Unilever had significant weekly sales data on mom and pop shops, which are generally informally run, and often run by women. We also discovered that some distributors provided access to credit, but this was not consistent.

To create an opportunity, we brought in a Mastercard bank partner, and were able to digitize the sales data from Unilever. The bank was able to extend credit to these mom and pop shops, which for the owners created access to the formal banking system and established a credit history—in many cases—for the first time. The shop owners as they grew their business could in turn also have access to other borrowing opportunities from the bank such as a mortgage loan.

Importantly, this scenario established a need on "why" a shop owner would want to participate in the financial system and brought increased revenue opportunities to Unilever and the bank.

This program with Unilever was launched in Kenya. 88% of the overall participants, and 94% of the female participants, reported that they increased sales in the first 6 months through access to credit. Additionally, 75% of the women reported that access to credit created a change in the level of respect in their household and the ability to make joint financial decisions at home. 94% of the women also reported a better quality of life.

In tandem to the access to credit, Mastercard also created a modular training program for the shop owners to understand how to use credit responsibly. This was an important consideration to marry the financial education with the access to credit programs, as well as create a framework that is replicable and scalable in other geographies. Mastercard plans to roll out the same program in Asia.

Moderator: *What is the "nudge" that is needed in the market to make investing in women's economic empowerment more attractive?*

Soukamneuth, Investing in Women: We see investing in women as not only the right thing to do, but the smart thing to do.

There are three areas where Impact investors find an interest to invest with a Gender Lens focus:
- Women generally control about 80% of the household income; impact investors have an interest to engage and better understand the group that controls the household monies.
- For impact investors, gender lens investing can be a natural extension, as they both consider social impact alongside the financial bottom line.
- Gender lens investing can be a "stepping stone" to increase the number of donors and reach more capital.

Moderator: *Do you have examples around pilots and market testing?*

Roman Tayag, BSP: A few examples include:

BSP has interest in the fast-moving consumer goods segment, reviewing their supply chains to see how they can digitize payments and create bespoke financial services for the financially underserved merchants.

One of the commercial banks in the Philippines was able to make a discovery by reviewing existing, female bank account holders. They learned that about one quarter of these account holders were business owners and were able to offer more relevant financial services to this target group.

Also, BSP has a sandbox that allows companies to "test" financial services offerings that do not fall under current regulations. This incubator provides great learning for BSP and can positively influence regulatory amendments.

Moderator: *Diversity and Inclusion is a topic beyond gender focus. How does Mastercard view the diversity and inclusion topic?*

Eskesen, Mastercard: Mastercard is very focused on gender parity around pay, career and voice. Diversity is driven from the chief executive officer level, and embraces diversity not only on gender, but also religion, age and other personal preferences. Mastercard is a great place to work!

An interesting example to share is a corporate social responsibility partnership with Levi Strauss and Marks and Spencer to explore women's economic empowerment.

Given the research evidence that digital payroll has a high likelihood to lead to increased savings and the ability to weather financial shocks, we explored digital payroll in the garment factory industry, which is dominated by female employees.

Our assessment revealed that factory payroll was generally once a month and paid in cash. This was a high cost to the employer to disburse these cash payments due to the logistics and security required. As pay day was a known date, this also created a security risk for the women to physically carry the cash home, and in many cases the factory workers' husbands were outside the factory gates to take the women's cash on pay day.

Another research-based learning is that women spend money differently than men and focus more spending on health and education costs.

It was understood that shifting pay from cash-based to digital payroll for female garment workers would impact the current practice of how these wages were received and handled within the household, which could cause issues between married partners. As a result, there was training (tools and role playing) before the digital payroll started that addressed the changes that may take place within the household as the woman would have more control over the digital receipt of her wages, and thus have more control over the spending of the wages.

Like other Mastercard programs, there is an understanding that financial education is an important part of the successful adoption to new financial services.

SPECIAL EVENT
Policy Dialogue on Leveraging Technology and Innovation for Disaster Risk Management and Financing

WELCOME REMARKS
Yasuyuki Sawada, Chief Economist and Director General, Economic Research and Regional Cooperation Department, Asian Development Bank (ADB)

Session 1: Presentation and discussion of the draft report

MODERATOR:
Yasuyuki Sawada, ADB

SPEAKERS:
Oliver Walker, Principal, Natural Resources Practice Lead, Vivid Economics

Leigh Wolfrom, Policy Analyst (Insurance), Directorate for Financial and Enterprise Affairs, Organisation for Economic Cooperation and Development (OECD)

Session 2: Policy Dialogue

MODERATOR:
Mamiko Yokoi-Arai, Head of Insurance, Directorate for Financial and Enterprise Affairs, OECD

SPEAKERS:
Sonu Agrawal, Founder and Managing Director, Weather Risk Management Services Private Limited

Paola Alvarez, Assistant Secretary, Department of Finance, Philippines

Guillermo Luz, Chief Resilience Officer and Advisor, Philippine Disaster Resilience Foundation, ABAC

Wei-Sen Li, Scientific Committee Member, Integrated Research on Disaster Risk (IRDR)

Thomas Kessler, Principal Finance Specialist (Disaster Insurance), Sustainable Development and Climate Change Department, ADB

CLOSING REMARKS:
Junkyu Lee, Chief of Finance Sector Group, Sustainable Development and Climate Change Department, ADB

The session discussed the initial findings of a joint report by ADB and the OECD , which is prepared under the Asia-Pacific Economic Cooperation (APEC) Finance Ministers' Process. The report examines how to leverage emerging technologies and innovation to improve disaster risk management and financing.

Since 2000, APEC economies have faced about $2.6 trillion in economic losses and 480,000 fatalities from significant natural hazard events, accounting for more than 40% of all victims and over 80% of economic losses reported globally. The region is particularly vulnerable to a wide range of natural hazards and extreme weather events and rising sea levels threaten the long-term viability of many Pacific islands. Moreover, climate change, population growth, and rapid economic development are expected to compound the social, economic, and financial impacts of natural hazards, threatening to undermine socioeconomic advancement and derail hard-won development gains.

To that end, ADB and the OECD have been collaborating on a joint report on leveraging technology and innovation for disaster risk management and financing. This is being undertaken in accordance with the APEC 2019 Finance Ministers' Process Work Plan.

In recognition of the importance of disaster risks, the APEC Finance Ministers agreed in the Cebu Action Plan to enhance financial resilience against economic shocks, including by "developing innovative disaster risk financing and insurance mechanisms (including micro-insurance) to enable APEC economies exposed to natural hazards to increase their financial response to disasters and reduce their fiscal burden."

This session shared the initial findings of the report and discussants offered further details from their own country perspectives.

The session highlighted that managing the social, economic, and financial impacts of natural hazards present a complex policy challenge for governments. Inadequate levels of risk awareness, insufficient integration of risk into strategic planning and investment decisions, and limited resources for investing in disaster risk reduction, emergency preparedness and response amplify the impact of natural hazard events.

Promisingly, however, emerging technologies and innovations can help improve disaster risk management and enhance the availability and affordability of financial protection. The report identified several promising areas. These included new sources of data (such as Earth observation sources), Internet of Things-connected devices, and social media (crowdsourcing); as well as data analysis and processing capacities such as artificial intelligence/machine learning, cloud computing, and spatial analysis tools.

Emerging technologies and innovation may also provide more effective communication tools such as mobile apps, social media, and web-based platforms that can support faster and more accessible dissemination of risk and impact information and mitigation and preparedness advice.

The report noted that the successful application of emerging technologies to disaster risk management and financing will require efforts to create an enabling environment. This is particularly so in five key areas: resilient and continuously improving telecommunications infrastructure, technical skills and capability, access to data and software, user awareness and acceptance, and regulatory adaptation.

The report also identified several areas policy makers can focus on in order to achieve these goals. Among these, promoting and supporting the application of emerging technologies and innovation as a policy goal in disaster risk management and financing is highlighted. This can be achieved by identifying innovation as a distinct objective of national disaster risk management and financing strategies. Offering specific funding for innovation through the establishment and funding of incubators targeted at the integration of new technologies; and funding training and partnerships to build local capacity amongst not only policymakers and regulators, but also practitioners on the ground can further advance shared goals.

The report underlined the importance of supporting education and awareness campaigns for users of technology and financial services to raise public awareness of disaster risks, disseminate best practices and tools that reduce vulnerability and exposure, and improve financial and insurance literacy.

The report also called for adapting regulatory frameworks for a digital environment. It called for establishing or adapting regulatory frameworks on the permissible use of data that will ensure sufficient privacy protection (accounting for potential differences in societal preferences for data protection), while also allowing for the use of data in disaster risk management and financing.

It also highlighted the need for adapting insurance (and potentially other financial sector) regulatory frameworks to allow for the development and dissemination of innovative financial protection products (such as parametric or index-based insurance) and to create appropriate incentives for disaster risk reduction activities and knowledge-sharing partnerships within the insurance sector – while maintaining public trust in financial protection products and providers.

SPECIAL EVENT
AgriFin Innovation Challenge

To help boost the productivity of the agriculture sector, the AgriFin Innovation Challenge was launched for fintech startups. The Challenge aimed to develop a digitized end-to-end ecosystem of varied solutions addressing smallholder farmer needs tied in by digital financial service.

More than 30 entries coming from various parts of the world were received and evaluated. The top three teams were then invited to Manila to deliver their final pitch. The winning team was awarded $10,000.

Finalists:
- Registered in Singapore but with initial operations in the Philippines, Asenso is an end-to-end micro, small and medium enterprise business accelerator fueling inclusive, last-mile growth for Asian firms. The company was established in 2019.
- FarmTrek is a solution of InfoCorp Technologies, an integrated FinTech and AgriTech company that aims to bring inclusive financial services to the livestock industry in emerging markets. InfoCorp was founded in 2015 with headquarters in Singapore.
- Tanijoy builds an agricultural ecosystem where farmers can be more independent, collaborative and interconnected through technology. The company is based in Sudirman, South Jakarta and was established in 2017.

MAIN FORUM

WELCOME ADDRESS

Bambang Susantono
Vice-President, Knowledge Management
and Sustainable Development

Good morning ladies and gentlemen and thank you for coming to this third annual Asia Finance Forum. Special thanks should also go to our important partners in the forum: the Government of Luxembourg and the Asian Development Bank (ADB) Institute. I extend special gratitude to all of you who have travelled to join us here.

Most of you here—policy makers and financial sector regulators, financial institutions, fintech companies, and academia from around the world—could agree that we are in an era of remarkable technological advances. There is an enormous opportunity to develop the financial services industry to reach some 1.7 billion people who remain "unbanked." Many of them are here in Asia and the Pacific.

We aim in this conference to build the capabilities of developing member countries and help prepare them for the wave of new digital technologies that are emerging in financial services.

There are many technological advances which have the potential to efficiently address long-standing obstacles and make real progress in expanding financial access. They include:
1. technologies applied in the context of regulatory sandboxes for testing financial innovations;
2. distributed ledger technology such as blockchain; and
3. digital identification (ID) establishment through the use of biometrics.

Yet, we must also be aware of the potential risks these new technologies bring. According to Financial Stability Board (2017), for example, risks from financial sources may include maturity mismatches, liquidity mismatches, and excess leverage. Operational risks may encompass, among others, cybersecurity, legal and regulatory challenges, and anti-money laundering or terrorist financing.

There are other systemwide vulnerabilities that can amplify shocks to the entire financial system. These risks are largely related to interactions between firms, investors, and clients that create important transmission channels and increase the likelihood of financial instability across the economy.

Indeed, failure to prepare for either the benefits or the risks could mean that poor and marginalized communities would likely be left even further behind as technology marches forward. It is important to strike a balance between pursuing benefits and mitigating potential risks, while creating an environment that embraces creativity and innovation.

In keeping with the goals of our overarching Strategy 2030, ADB is experimenting with leading edge initiatives to apply digital technologies, especially in the finance sector. The overarching aim is to efficiently increase access to finance for all, including the marginalized.

For example, yesterday ADB conducted one of our Hackathon Challenges that aimed to provide fintech solutions to address the needs of the agriculture sector. The Hackathon Challenge is a series of activities to which we invite the startup community to submit "Agtech" and fintech solutions that may potentially be piloted as operational projects in one of our developing member countries. We observed very creative and savvy solutions from blockchain for livestock management to the use of geographic information systems for crop insurance.

If these solutions are deemed successful, farmers who represent a high share in the unbanked population can start gaining greater access to financial tools, thereby gaining more economic empowerment.

Indeed, ADB has been working on expanding innovative financial services through our projects and technical assistance as well.

The first example is from Bangladesh. We completed last year a weather index-based crop insurance pilot in three districts, involving over 9,500 smallholder rice farmers. Crop insurance is particularly valuable today when the effects of climate change are making farming more unpredictable. It can be called a climate adaptation tool, as it offers farmers the capacity to plan and put aside some money to cope with difficult times when harvests are suddenly damaged or destroyed. Crop insurance also allows farmers to invest in modern technology that lifts productivity and incomes.

This $2 million grant project featured innovative components that included (i) the use of mobile banking services for the collection of insurance premiums and payment of claims; (ii) development of parametric weather indices for claims settlement without on-the-spot assessment of crop damages, following excess or deficit rainfall; and (iii) the installation of automated weather stations for providing climate-related information.

The second example is from here in the Philippines. Some of you have probably heard of our support to Cantilan Bank's launch of cloud-based core banking services. In coordination with the Philippine Central Bank, Cantilan piloted cloud technology testing in its regulatory sandbox. Cantilan Bank's core banking system was recently fully migrated to the cloud and has won several awards, including: Digital Trailblazer for Financial Services award from the Bangko Sentral ng Pilipinas and finalist for Outstanding Partner for Digital Transformation.

Cloud technology for core banking brings immense value to financial institutions such as Cantilan Bank. With this capability:
- The bank can now reach the underserved and unbanked in a more efficient manner through their mobile/tablet solution.
- It can offer the clients new opportunities to save funds, make payments, get a small business loan, send remittances, or buy insurance.

- It provides personalized and efficient services even in remote locations.
- It can mitigate various strategic and operational information technology (IT) risks and reduce major IT capital expenses.

Cantilan Bank is the first bank in the Philippines to use high level technology in this way.

Allow me to give one more ADB project example of digital technology application, this one from Papua New Guinea—a country where some 85% of the low-income population reportedly has no access to formal financial services. This project, Digital Access Tool through biometric ID, is supporting the country's MiBank and Women's Microbank provide financial services to low-income and financially underserved people in remote areas.
- The biometric ID will allow people to verify personal attributes such as name, gender and biometrics and thus access financial services safely and securely. This will aid considerably in establishing know your customer (KYC) information, which, we all know is critical to accessing financial services.
- The tool will use smart cards on standard Android mobile phones.
- This smart card-based digital access tool works without power and internet, which is important for reaching unbanked people in the remotest locations.

The overall aim of the project is to make those people become more visible, more bankable, and have a better chance to move out of poverty.

Distinguished guests, ladies and gentlemen,
Our program today and tomorrow is an opportunity to explore together what more we can do—we must do—to further the financial inclusion agenda, by leveraging new technology. We want to get down to the specifics of how the poor and the unbanked, including women and small businesses, can be empowered through adoption of new technology in the finance sector.

At the same time, we also need to ensure that information security, data, consumer protection, and financial stability are at the center of preparation for digital financial services.

The need to harness the power of technology is also attributed to the fact that financial markets in Asia and the Pacific are becoming increasingly interconnected with global and regional financial markets. Digital technology will further speed up the potential spread of contagion between markets. Time is ripe, therefore, to take quick and innovative policy measures to increase the potential for positive cross-border spillovers and guard against unintended consequences.

This brings me to stress how important it is for an event like this forum to bring experts and policy makers together and contribute to regional knowledge-sharing efforts and policy dialogues to address challenges of fintech operations.

I would like to highlight in this regard that ADB has been contributing to this important dialogue and knowledge sharing by conducting research and publishing policy papers, ranging from country-specific analyses to broader sector reports.

For example, we have published this year Pacific Finance Sector Briefs for each country in the Asia and the Pacific region. We are also increasing the number of working papers and reports, not only broadly on the finance sector and financial inclusion, but more specifically on fintech in Asia and the Pacific. All of these reports are available online from our ADB website.

I would like to conclude my remarks with ADB's commitment to continue supporting our member countries tap full potential of digital technologies so our children can enjoy productive and safe digital lives. No one should be left behind in this digital economy.

This Third Asia Finance Forum is an exciting opportunity to advance our understanding on these new technologies. Once again, thank you for coming and I wish you a productive conference.

Thank you.

The Digital Revolution: Access to Finance for All

Rama Sridhar, Executive Vice President, Mastercard

Rama Sridhar began her keynote address by stating that while it is often said that we have entered the age of the Fourth Industrial Revolution—an era that, in the words of one writer, "builds and extends the impact of digitization in new and unanticipated ways," this is not the case for hundreds of millions of people, most of whom are poor and live in the developing world.

Disruptive and transformative advances in technology, education, health and finance that have taken place in the developed world have created new industries and reshaped old ones impacting and transforming large chunks of the society.

However, she strongly emphasized that the Digital Revolution will not automatically ensure access to finance for all. There needs to be a comprehensive action plan with a quantified outcome that is fueled by the growth of the information and communications technology (ICT) sector and other building blocks, along with a targeted focus on financially excluded population pools and an understanding of their needs.

The Role of the ICT Sector

The ICT sector is particularly important, contributing 5%–10% of the gross domestic product (GDP) of many developed countries. It is even more important to many middle-income countries, where the ICT sector can rank in the top 3 industries.

But Sridhar stressed that this is just part of the story. The impact of the ICT sector is relatively small compared to the benefits when technology is adopted across economies. It's not about just building a thriving ICT sector, it is about driving digitization throughout society.

Making a comparison of the ICT sector in the United States, Viet Nam and India, the ICT sector in the United States accounts for about 8% of GDP. At the same time, the United States has embraced digitization and ranks 15th in the world in ICT adoption and 8th in GDP per capita.

Comparatively, while ICT makes up about 40% of Viet Nam's GDP, the country has not embraced a digital economy. Viet Nam ranks 131 in nominal GDP per capita, and 108 in the United Nation's ICT Development Index, which measures internet access, use and skills. Viet Nam could generate over $100 billion in incremental wealth by 2045 if Vietnamese society embraces digitization in the same way the United States has done.

India is a similar story. While the country is the world's second largest exporter of ICT, it ranked 121 in GDP per capita and 138 in internet development. India has already started the digitization journey; the issuance of the Aadhaar identification card is a remarkable example. According to McKinsey, digitization could generate $1 trillion in growth in India by 2025.

In summary, countries which rank poorly in the United Nation's Internet Development Index also have low GDP per capita; Asian countries fall very closely to this trendline. There is a direct correlation between a country's digital adoption and GDP per capita. This is because of the gains in productivity and innovation that digitization unlocks.

Six Building Blocks of Digital Dividends

While ICT adoption is a prerequisite to realizing digital dividends, it is just one of the building blocks of digital transformation. ICT adoption must be accompanied by trust, user identification, financial enablement, security and a regulatory framework which enables growth.

Sridhar commented on many digital businesses such as Yahoo, eBay and Uber exemplify digitization's capacity to increase the number and quality of interactions that we have, and yet they have struggled with many of these building blocks to deliver trusted payments in their company growth.

The Digital Revolution Risks Leaving Millions Behind

Sridhar asked the audience to consider how digitization could create financial access for target population groups. The first focus group is the 1.7 billion people outside of the formal financial system; more than half of this group lives in Asia and the Pacific. These "financially excluded" people pay high fees and trust risky systems for simple transactions, rely on cash or barter for necessities, and are locked out of technological advances and advantages.

Sridhar highlighted that Mastercard looks at financial inclusion more broadly, adding a focus on millions of micro, small and medium enterprises that are outside of the formal financial system. Mastercard also focuses on the billions of people who are in the formal banking and financial system, but who need help in order to persuade them that going digital won't see them fall victim to issues such as cybercrime, tracking and identify theft.

The scale of digital financial exclusion is profound. World Bank's Global Findex Database 2017 research showed that more than 90% of people in India, Myanmar, Sri Lanka, Cambodia, and the Lao People's Democratic Republic had never used the internet to make a bill payment or shop online. The proportion was only slightly lower in the Philippines and Indonesia.

What is needed to counter financial exclusion? The solution lies in greater ICT access, trust and regulatory action to achieve three main goals: reducing socio-economic barriers, extending accessibility of broadband infrastructure, and addressing digital skills gaps.

In the Asia-Pacific region, small and medium-sized enterprises comprise 95% of all enterprises, employ half of the workforce, and contribute between 20% and 50% of countries' GDPs. Worldwide, formal MSMEs face a funding gap of $5.2 trillion, more than half of that gap is in the East Asia and Pacific region.

In large part, this gap exists because it is difficult and costly for the large banks that control capital investments in emerging markets to assess small firms' creditworthiness. SMEs need easier access to capital, need to get paid on time, and need to ensure that digital payments are seamlessly integrated into doing business. The good news is that digitization is helping with all three issues.

Sridhar cited examples of the fast growth of alternative financing in Asia with multiple options ranging from peer-to-peer business-lending to invoice factoring and equity-based crowdfunding. Indonesia's Akseleran demonstrates that alternative financing should not be deemed risky. Its ratio of non-performing loans is 0.5% compared to the 3% national average. Among its loan products, Akseleran offers SMEs up to 80% of the value of their receivables for up to three months.

Tackling digital phobia for the financially included population is the 3rd focus for Mastercard. Today in India, Thailand, Malaysia, Philippines and Indonesia, most e-commerce orders are still paid via cash-on-delivery arrangements. To combat the lack of trust to make a digital payment, consumers must be able to trust that the payment ecosystem providers provide have a three-prong approach: protect all personal and private information, process all digital transactions in a secure manner and defend against cyber-attackers.

The Future of Inclusive Finance

Sridhar closed the keynote address by citing that the impact of a fully realized digital dividend is estimated to add more than $1 trillion to the GDPs of Association of Southeast Asian Nations countries by 2025, and that combined with India, this represents a staggering $2 in potential dividends in the region.

However, she reminded again that internet access isn't enough. All the building blocks must be present for people to share ideas, to innovate, to buy and sell, and ultimately make the transactions that are quantified by the definition of GDP.

Mastercard is expert at facilitating digital transactions that lead to the exchange of value across ecosystems. The company uses the building blocks of trust, authentication, security of information and transactions, working with regulators to create appropriate growth frameworks, and of course, digitizing finance and payments. As examples, in the Philippines, the national switch BancNet is working with Mastercard to leapfrog several generations of payment technology in bringing the country to the forefront of real-time payment infrastructure. In Australia, Mastercard is working with the government to create an ID program.

On a final note, Ms Sridhar stated that the race towards digital democracy has just started. We are far from the finish line. No one should be left behind.

SESSION 1
Inclusive Finance: Combining Fintech Innovation, Public–Private Collaboration, and Responsive Regulation to Reach the Poorest

MODERATOR:
Robin Newnham, Head of Policy Analysis, Alliance for Financial Inclusion

PANELISTS:

Heidi Echtermann-Toribio, Managing Director and Global Head, Financial Institutions, Standard Chartered Bank

Xiaowen (Sherwin) Pu, Principal Investment Specialist, Private Sector Operations Department, Asian Development Bank (ADB)

Pia Roman Tayag, Managing Director, Center for Learning and Inclusion Advocacy, Bangko Sentral ng Pilipinas (BSP)

Mahmood Sattar, Board Director, BRAC Bank and Board Director, bKash Limited

What is next in digital financial services technologies that meet the needs at the base of pyramid? How do you locate and reach these new customers? How can digital financial services bridge the gap to the underserved poor?

Learn about reaching underserved and untapped markets.

The Moderator, Robin Newnham of the Alliance for Financial Inclusion, kicked off the session by presenting the landscape on financial inclusion.

Robin Newnham—Opening Remarks

Financial inclusion and technology innovation go almost hand in glove. We simply cannot dream of achieving "inclusive financial systems for all" without taking advantage of the breakthroughs seen in technology innovation. This has been evident as far back as the development of M-pesa in Kenya, the first mobile money scheme 12 years ago, which allowed unbanked Kenyans to make payments by feature phones, and now allows access to a full range of credit, saving, insurance other financial products.

We've seen similar mobile money schemes take off across Africa, Asia and Latin America, but other technology innovations have also proven to be game changers for financial inclusion. We've seen agent banking rollouts that have taken financial services into the deepest reaches of the Amazon in Brazil or in Borneo in Malaysia. We have seen biometric technologies allow more than a billion people in India to have a unique identity and use that identity to remotely open bank accounts and conduct other financial services.

Equally important to the technology innovation with financial inclusion has been the progress of regulatory and the policy innovation that has really met it.

More than 150 countries in the world now have established and launched a National Financial Inclusion strategy. A total of 68 countries have set together that more than 700 quantified targets for financial inclusion under the framework known as the Maya Declaration and more than 30 countries now have launched regulatory sandboxes building on those early "test and learn" approaches of central banks. The number of unbanked has now been reduced to 1.7 billion people.

We are witnessing a wider range of technologies including cloud computing, artificial intelligence, distributed ledger technologies, and advanced data analytics just to name a few. We are also witnessing an ever-increasing range of players entering the financial services space, no longer limited to brick-and-mortar institutions like banks and microfinance institutions.

We can also see fintechs that are emerging offering greater value and convenience to their customers. Ride-hailing companies are building on their data and offering financial services such as payments and credit. Technology giants such as Ant Financial and Tencent in the People's Republic of China that have become the default channels for making digital payments in those markets, but I think in the last couple of years, we are also seeing some changes in how fintechs are perceived.

A few years ago, we talked about fintechs as some sort of digital barbarians at the gate, disrupting the established order and maybe cherry-picking the most profitable and least regulated financial services activities. Today there is a lot less talk about disruption and the "end of banks," and a lot more talk about the collaboration possibilities and about developing fintech ecosystems. Within this ecosystem, we are now seeking ways to collaborate and achieve a healthy equilibrium.

Panel Session

Moderator (question to panel): How do you see the development of fintech ecosystems and how is your organization collaborating with the goal of financial inclusion in mind?

Heidi Echtermann-Toribio: The topic of fintech ecosystems is an important one. While five years ago the focus was on disruption to banks, the conversation has moved on to one of exploration and understanding of what this opportunity can bring to banks and our customers across many geographies. There is now a focus on collaboration with fintechs, and how we can create customized solutions with a targeted approach.

Sherwin Pu: ADB supports fintechs through its public sector work such as government policy and regulatory dialogue, including a focus on fintech ecosystems. ADB has also recently set up ADB Ventures, which is a first-time initiative to systematically invest in start-up companies. Fintechs are one of the main verticals of ADB Ventures, and through this vertical, we will support the base of the pyramid.

Pia Roman-Tayag: BSP takes a collaborative, public-private sector approach as a regulator with our regulated institutions. The first focus is mindset, an openness and flexibility to the approach to new financial services activities. Today only 30% of Filipinos are banked, so there is a need for more solutions, models and technologies to address this issue. The "test and learn"/ sandbox approach has been used for the private sector to experiment, and BSP keeps good communication with the private sector to ensure risk-appropriate regulation.

As a second area, BSP has also partnered beyond regulatory matters with several institutions on the important topic of financial education and consumer protection. The last area of collaboration is across jurisdictions with the understanding that to achieve financial inclusion through the BSP's Financial Inclusion Strategy it will require the cooperation of many public sector and private sector groups. This approach cuts across the central bank, securities and exchange commission and the insurance commission who regulate fintechs and provide strategic guidance from the government in their planning.

BSP views this collaborative approach to be enabling and creating a sustainable environment that protects consumers.

Mahmood Sattar: Bangladesh is very well known as the first market outside of Africa where mobile money really ignited and became a major driver of financial inclusion. Mobile money started in Bangladesh in 2010. Since then there have only been a few companies such as bKash that has significant market share; banks are only now catching up.

On public–private partnerships, the Bangladesh government formed a2i (access to information). Today citizens need not travel more than 4 kilometers to access more than 150 services at their village digital center.

Fintechs started to arrive in Bangladesh about 3–4 years ago, they especially started to add value in the area of payments for online transactions. While today people in Bangladesh are starting to use e-commerce, it is primarily using cash on delivery.

While there is a process to link credit and debit cards to e-commerce, this only reaches a limited number of citizens. Mobile money operators, such as bKash and Rocket, have an e-KYC (know your customer) and approval process that is less stringent compared to a bank account or credit card. They have a larger reach to the masses as a payment mechanism and can be linked to e-commerce and other services.

In October 2019, three digital one-stop services were launched—Eksheba, Ekpay and Ekshop—to enable Bangladesh citizens to get different government services, pay utility bills and other fees, as well as engage in e-commerce activities. This is an a2i program under the information and communication technology division, who will implement these services.

Moderator: How have banks collaborated with fintechs, and how has it enabled reach to the unbanked and underserved?

Echtermann-Toribio: One of the most exciting things that we're working on today is how we connect with fintechs. As an example, Standard Chartered Ventures invests seed capital in young companies, and can create sandbox environments for fintechs to explore new opportunities and ideas.

KYC can be quite onerous in some countries, and when moving funds cross border, it becomes more complex. Standard Chartered is working on how we can partner with other financial institutions and regulators to set an international standard to move funds more rapidly. As an example, the bank did some work with Ant Financial on remittance flows from Hong Kong, China to the Philippines.

Standard Chartered also has a view that we can be a building block with tech partners to serve communities where we operate. In all markets, financial literacy is imperative, as well as gaining the customer's trust through the relevant payment methods and financial services.

Moderator: How can we improve regulatory standards in the fintech sector?

Pu: Development banks can play a role to ensure that inclusion is a part of regulatory standards. A complicated standard that relies on a digital solution may not fit areas of countries that do not have reliable infrastructure such as electricity or mobile connectivity.

Roman-Tayag: There must be some basic standards to cover technology risk management, financial integrity and consumer protection. However, there cannot be a "one size fits all"; standards must be commensurate with the size and complexity of the business model but there are some very basic prerequisites that do need to be met.

Also, challenges arise when there are different types of financial institutions across different regulators for example a more activity-based view on standards for consistency.

Sattar: Fintechs may want to have fewer standards imposed on their services to enable them to more efficiently reach and engage with the financially underserved. In Bangladesh, there is the advantage that everyone has a national identification as a starting point of KYC.

By capping the transaction values of fintech services there can be proportionate standards for the risk of new fintechs offering services to people whose financial literacy may not be high.

Moderator: On remittances, why has it been difficult to bring costs down? Do you see any promising breakthroughs on the horizon from the latest wave of innovation and partnerships?

Roman-Tayag: Remittances are very important to the Philippine economy, and there has been progress made to bring costs down. Cost reduction has occurred as a result of the multiplicity of players, last-mile options, and technology.

To refocus the question, there is a bigger issue which is what remittance recipients do with the funds received from overseas. For example, if the remittance is received into a bank account, is the bank account also used to make digital purchases, or access other services of the bank? Understanding how remittances are used is a nascent area with more potential to have a multiplier effect to improve the welfare of beneficiaries. BSP is looking to conduct pilots to see how new technology can make an impact.

Echtermann-Toribio: Standard Chartered has been doing work in the remittance space and working with fintechs. However, not all fintechs were able to achieve cost reductions for remittances.

An area of focus should be the sender and receiver and ensuring the safety of the remittance methodologies. For example, some e-wallets used on either side of the remittance transaction may not be insured. There needs to be strong financial education and consumer protection around remittances.

Sattar: Remittance senders focus on two product features: speed to delivery and low cost. The remittance value size coming into the Philippines is generally higher as their job levels are higher compared to Bangladesh and other South Asian countries.

Generally, bank to bank transfers are expensive, as well as global remittance operators such as Western Union and Moneygram.

For remittance receivers in Bangladesh, there is a benefit to receive the funds into a m-wallet of one of the 16 mobile financial services (MFS) providers such as bKash, Rocket, or iPay as the cost is less expensive, and they can digitally pay from the mobile wallet to make purchases, pay utilities and pay taxes.

Moderator: Question to the Philippines: How do you manage risk, innovation and financial stability while managing the goal of reaching the unbanked? Mindset has been mentioned, so how can we encourage people to use new technology and trust the new services?

Roman-Tayag: The BSP is very focused on understanding the market, we have a regular financial inclusion survey, and we use an evidence-based approach in what we will promote, where the gaps are, and what policy needs to be put in place. That is how we are balancing the needs of the market with more responsive regulations.

Moderator: What is the state of play with third-party aggregators in Bangladesh?

Sattar: This is still a nascent area and has room to grow. Remittances has been a focus area for Bangladesh, especially to drive down costs for operators and migrant workers.

Bangladesh Bank has issued a notification that as of January 2020 that there will be interoperability between MFS operators and banks; this will allow smaller MFS operators to more efficiently participate in the market. The service would be settled by the National Payment Switch of Bangladesh Bank.

There are five types of payment providers: banks, non-bank financial institutions, MFS providers, payment service providers and payment service operators. Aggregators should benefit by the central bank's notification of interoperability between MFS operators and banks.

Moderator: Should banks just focus on the back office and fintechs on the front office?

Echtermann-Toribio: Standard Chartered does partner with a lot of fintechs to see how we can reach a wider audience, where they use our technology and infrastructure to ensure a safe environment. I think this is a model that you will see more going forward.

When there is a comment "that banks are a hurdle," it is most likely due to our policies and processes to protect the financial services industry and all of its millions of customers. It is estimated that there is over $1.5 trillion of illicit funds that flows through the financial services industry every year. As banks collaborate with fintech partners, we can help to facilitate good banking practices in the industry and work towards reducing costs while ensuring safe delivery of payments.

Moderator: What is ADB Ventures' risk appetite? Will ADB Ventures consider a pilot project in one of the Pacific Island states?

Pu: Initially, ADB Ventures will invest in early stage start-ups, from Pre-Series A to Series A. We will invest in companies that are about to make revenue, have established a business model, have a prototype, and are ready to launch a business. We would like to help these companies with pilot testing and provide a sum of funding to take them to the next step.

The ADB Ventures program will expand beyond this initial phase, based on market demand.

ADB Ventures can do projects in the Pacific Islands. We are currently doing a CleanTech pilot project in Papua New Guinea.

Moderator: Does the Philippines allow for virtual/digital banks? Does the Philippines have a digital ID/KYC scheme?

The BSP has approved digital banks but only for traditional banks that have opted to have a digital-only presence in the Philippines. There are purely digital banks in the pipeline, but regulations do not currently provide for that business model; this is under review.

National ID is very important to fintech and financial inclusion agendas. The Philippines does not have a national ID. However, last year a national ID law was put in place, similar to the national ID program that was rolled out in India. A national ID in the Philippines will be very important for leveraging access to financial services, access to credit, opening bank accounts, and KYC.

Moderator: Asking each panelist for a final takeaway on what is critical for an inclusive fintech ecosystem to succeed.

Echtermann-Toribio: The more that we can focus on collaboration, the faster we can respond and accelerate this important initiative of financial inclusion.

Pu: Although inclusive fintech is a part of fintech, it is very difficult and needs the support of the technology sector and more innovation.

Roman-Tayag: Focus on the customer.

Sattar: Reach out [to the financially underserved and unbanked], provide them with relevant (digestible) solutions, and ensure that regulators and innovators deliver to a high standard.

Moderator—closing remarks: This has been a rich discussion. We have seen that the task of integrating technology in new actors into the financial system is challenging as pitfalls and risks to be navigated. There are enormous opportunities when it comes to the potential gains for financial inclusion and all sorts of other policy objectives as well.

The need for collaboration has come across very strongly in new forms of innovative partnerships. So, I think we can conclude by stating the well-known proverb that "we might move faster by going alone, but we're going to go a lot further by working together."

SESSION 2
Turning Financial Access into Actual Usage:
The Power of Financial Literacy

MODERATOR:
Lotte Schou-Zibell, Regional Director, Pacific Department, Asian Development Bank (ADB)

PANELISTS:

Hema Bansal, Senior Director, The Smart Campaign, Center for Financial Inclusion at Accion

Peter Morgan, Senior Consulting Economist and Vice Chair for Research, ADB Institute

Akshat Pathak, Senior Manager, Microsave Consulting

Grace Tan, Head of Corporate Communication, Visa Inc.

Lack of financial and digital literacy is a major reason for lack of access to finance for women and in rural communities. Policies to enhance financial inclusion, especially through technology, should involve more active financial literacy and educational programs.

Learn about new products and services, players, and channels that address the essential need of financial literacy to reach the underserved and unbanked and drive the shift from financial access to financial usage.

As the world evolves into a more digital and online environment, financial inclusion and literacy are going to be increasingly important. Despite significant investment in financial literacy training by many organizations, millions of people remain financially illiterate and excluded. This session discussed how to use financial literacy to expand financial access and usage.

Peter Morgan began by stressing a "potentially synergistic effect between fintech and financial literacy." Through work in the Lao People's Democratic Republic using the augmented adult financial literacy survey by the Organisation for Economic Co-operation and Development (OECD) and International Gateway for Financial Education that included questions about fintech knowledge and fintech use, "we did find a positive correlation between financial literacy and the use of fintech services."[1]

Similarly, a survey of financial literacy by the Bank of Japan with about 25,000 respondents showed a significant positive correlation between financial literacy and the use of fintech payment services.

Widening the discussion, Lotte Schou-Zibell asked "how can financial capabilities complement traditional financial literacy and how are you going to define or distinguish financial literacy and financial capability?"

"Financial capability basically integrates behavioral dimensions," noted Hema Bansal. "What differentiates financial literacy from capability is that with financial literacy you do not know whether it will lead to changes in behavior." With greater capability clients are more informed and able to take make more rational financial choices, a fundamental difference from simple literacy.

---

[1] OECD. 2016. OECD/INFE International Survey of Adult Financial Literacy Competencies. Paris.

She stressed that by imparting capability you instill knowledge and skills to a client as they do their transactions. It becomes a part of the process of the delivery of a financial product.

Bansal highlighted that the Center for Financial Inclusion, Accion has identified several behavioral practices that can change client behavior. The first focuses on "teachable moments," in which it is important to reach consumers when they are making financial decisions or signing up for her firm's financial services.

Second is learning by doing, which provides opportunities to clients to use technology. You can have simulations, for example women in Colombia were taught to become familiar with ATMs.

The third is "nudges," i.e., giving clients timely reminders to do desired behavior, whether by SMS or in person. For example, Green Bank in the Philippines used nudges to improve the saving behavior of its clients, after which clients' savings increased by 82% in 1 year.

Other principles include making it fun to learn, for example through games and chatbots that can communicate with people in local language to tailor a message to their audience. "If you make anything social it really works."

Nonetheless, sometimes the problem is getting people to use the knowledge they may have. "Even when we have seen huge improvement in creating access, the usage is still subpar. We have over 800 million registered mobile money accounts globally, but only 24% of them are active," Akshat Pathak pointed out. The same is true of bank accounts and other instruments. The challenge is not in a person's capability, it is in their intent to use it.

"Microsave has been targeting very basic problems," said Akshat Pathak. His firm is using a "case app framework" which focuses on knowledge, skills, abilities, and practice. To add to the principles shared by Bansal, he said that the entire experience must be easy to understand, "intuitive, based on their mental models; it has to be relatable to them and there has to be a concept of human touch."

Grace Tan shared some of her experiences at Visa and their work in the Philippines. She described her company's two-year financial literacy program, which was conducted in partnership with the Bangko Sentral ng Pilipinas, Tanghalang Pilipino, a theater production company, and Teach for the Philippines, a non-profit organization that reaches out to the country's teacher network.

"You have to teach it in a creative way, and the program has to be really relevant to the local community." The first phase incorporated financial literacy concepts that were scripted into a theater program, and produced in Tagalog. It was piloted, in local schools in Metro Manila. The company then decided to scale it up to help make the program more sustainable. In the second year, it decided to extend production beyond Metro Manila and it was produced in a soft copy format that could be shared through a USB.

"So, we worked with Teach for the Philippines and did training within their network. The teachers then deployed what they've learned into different areas in the Philippines and shared it with teachers in their own schools. We produced a teacher's manual where they could show the screenplay in the classrooms as part of life skills or financial literacy curriculum. The manual included step-by-step questions which could guide teachers to impart financial literacy in the classroom sessions. In the last two years, we've scaled the program and reached out to more than 35,000 students and teachers across the Philippines."

Grace added that the first challenge is the sustainability of the program. The second challenge is measurement of the longer-term impact, because you cannot just do a pre- and post-survey to determine how successful the program is. The ideal impact measurement from the program is to identify long-term behavioral changes among the participants.

The session also defined what digital literacy is. Morgan noted "the concept of digital financial literacy is the intersection between financial literacy and digital literacy, but it also goes beyond these." It includes several parts: knowledge of the various fintech products and services, knowledge of alternative sources of finance such as person-to-person lending or crowdfunding, knowledge of asset management such as robo advisors, and knowledge of products such as microinsurance and of the risks of those products.

SESSION 3
Breaking Barriers to Widen Financial Access through Innovation: Stories from the Field

MODERATOR:
Jost Wagner, Managing Director and Professional Facilitator, The Change Initiative Co., Ltd.

PANELISTS:
Nino Bigvava, Head of Project Management Department, FINCA Bank Georgia

Trudi Egi, Head of Mobile Banking, Nationwide Microbank Limited (MiBank)

Antonio Separovic, Chief Executive Officer and Co-founder, Oradian

Understand the highlights and pain points when introducing innovation to existing traditional financial services. Selected Asian Development Bank (ADB) pilot projects across Asia and the Pacific will be showcased to demonstrate development impacts, best practice, and innovation.

In this special session, with the aid of PowerPoint slides, panelists were each given just over six minutes to present the work they have been doing with ADB support to widen financial access through innovation.

Nino Bigvava, Head of Project Management Department, FINCA Bank Georgia: Nino Bigvava got the session under way with a look at her bank's pilot project using a digital field application and credit scoring to leverage digital technology and mobile financial services to bring faster, more reliable loan approval processes to communities in rural areas.

FINCA received its banking license in 2013 and has 35 branches serving over 100,000 customers, of which 20,000 are farmers and small entrepreneurs; 79% of clients are rural dwellers and 40% of approvals are for agricultural loans.

She said that credit loan officers conducted field visits where internet connectivity was very low, thus making it challenging to complete the 40 steps needed to finalize loan approvals, which they did using online and offline tools.

She said the bank was confident that it could decrease the average cost and duration of the loan approval process by a significant amount. Loan approval—conducted online and offline using mobile devices—on average takes about 97 minutes and costs €14.87.

"One outcome of this pilot project is to enhance local capacity of service providers, not only FINCA Bank, but other institutions will also benefit from less expensive financial solutions to expand the inclusion of farmers in financial services," she said.

Essentially, the process first involves three calls to loan applicants: one to filter out those with bad credit history or who do not otherwise meet the criteria, the second to adjust the market interest rate and pricing offer, the third to finalize approval.

The automated system allowed delivery of loan decisions to the small entrepreneurs quickly and at their places of business. All preparation and other factors are done by the bank. "All the changes, all the new requirements, are conducted on our side and we can build the application using hard and software validation to minimize the risks and to ensure all product requirements, international and local, are considered." This can be done because "we have integration with the third parties, with almost all digital governmental organizations providing the public information about the customer—national registry, public registry, etc." All the information is available in a couple of seconds and financial assessment is provided at the business location.

Trudi Egi, Head of Mobile Banking, MiBank: MiBank's digital access tool will enable provision of financial services to low-income and financially underserved people in remote areas of Papua New Guinea.

By bringing these people into the formal sector they can become more visible, more bankable, and have a better chance to move out of poverty. Some 85% of the low-income population reportedly has no access to formal financial services. The country is a signatory to the Maya Declarations, said Trudi Egi, and that has been "very supportive in us going out to rural areas to provide a financial inclusion and financial literacy program."

The bank has 150 staff in 10 branches and decided to go mobile using mobile money and mobile technology. The app, with agents in many parts of the country, provides cash-in cash-out services, micro-insurance, and solar pay as you go service.

In the remote, hard-to-reach areas of the mountainous country, the bank faces many challenges, including heavy rain or construction blocking access to rural areas. "You still need access to customers and those customers are very difficult to reach in areas like this."

Even when the weather is good it can be difficult to get cash to remote areas, with the firm resorting at times to helicopter drops at predetermined locations. Egi showed a picture of a small shed with a "funnel" on the roof big enough to receive the bag drop.

The digital access tool will allow low-income and underserved populations to verify personal attributes such as name, gender, and biometrics and thus access to financial services safely and securely with smart cards. This will aid considerably in establishing know-your-customer information, fundamental in obtaining access to financial services.

The operation's smart cards work with standard Android mobile phones as near field communication readers. Customers will only need their smart card, a digital access tool that can work without power and internet—once the digital access tool is in a connected area, information can then be synched to MiBank's information system.

The way it works is a customer arrives at a point of service and staff there read the customer card with a mobile device and check the person's identification (ID) with the information stored on the device. Authentication is initiated with a button to an online bank, the user provides a PIN, and a two-factor authentication is performed.

Antonio Separovic, Chief Executive Officer and Co-founder, Oradian: Oradian set out in 2012 to create a cloud-based toolset, starting in a rural region of northern Nigeria, that would allow them to reach customers in remote and unbanked regions to identify and address the challenges they face.

In partnership with Cantilan Bank in the Philippines it recently concluded a pilot project in Mindanao (southern Philippines) that fully migrated the bank's core banking system onto the cloud, making Cantilan the first bank in the Philippines to use high technology in this way. "This enables the financial institution to go deeper into hard-to-reach places," said Separovic.

"What really made this project special is that it's an important project for the central bank who set out a policy in 2013, Cantilan Bank being the first to embrace it." In addition, ADB provided important support to the central bank in addressing the impact of the change in policy.

An important part of Oradian's approach, he said, is "high tech, high touch."

"Without the high touch component, it's very difficult to deliver on the promise of financial inclusion. This means that we do the work with the institution to help it adapt to the change." He showed a picture of a crowded banking operation, overflowing with files and disorganization before Oradian got involved. After, a gleaming, modern, computer-based operation, access to information became quick and this freed people up in the institution to focus on its customers.

Our core banking system is as you usually expect, it has a loan savings portfolio. However, we go one step further where we work with financial institutions, we partner with them, (and) we build the community and share our know-how. So, we're a team of specialists who both provide the technology but work with the customers on an ongoing basis."

The firm starts by digitizing then optimizes processes and continues to grow, and that growth is through forming a community with customers. By the numbers, as of August 2019, the company portfolio value grew from 10% to 150%, end-clients served grew from 30% to 200%, and branch growth increased from 4% to 200%.

Globally, the company has achieved this in 12 countries and is servicing 80 financial institutions, reaching four million end-clients on its platform.

SESSION 4A
Going Cashless: The Importance of Interoperable Payment Systems

MODERATOR:
Thomas Abell, Advisor and Chief of Digital Technology for Development, Sustainable Development and Climate Change Department, Asian Development Bank (ADB)

PANELISTS:

Joseph Chan, Undersecretary, Financial Services and the Treasury, Hong Kong, China

Sang-seung Oh, Head, Global Business Team, Korea Financial Telecommunications and Clearings Institute

Richa Pant, Head, Corporate Social Responsibility, L&T Financial Services

Tricia Cuna Weaver, Vice President, Paysys Global LLC

Interoperability enables people to make payments to anyone, any time in a convenient, affordable, fast, seamless and secure way via a single transaction account and using any device. This means that a customer need only maintain one account—a bank or an e-money account— to be able to conveniently and affordably transact with anyone in the system.

Learn how a pro-poor payment system should be built on the principles of interoperability, inclusivity, cooperation, and competition.

The potential for the sort of financial disruption that can allow countries to move toward digitally delivered systems and away from cash—going cashless— is significantly magnified by the existence of an interoperable payment system. This was among the major points made in this session, which viewed the issue from several perspectives.

Indeed, one panelist, Tricia Cuna Weaver, likened the existence of national-level, real-time, interoperable payment systems to the internet. Google and other technology companies did not have to build their own internet to begin offering their services; the essential infrastructure was already there promoting market efficiencies and allowing these companies to compete on base products and services rather than on infrastructure.

Yet, among the significant problems in broadening access to financial services is that such infrastructure, which is necessary for financial inclusion, is not in place.

The moderator opened the session asking: "What are the regulatory requirements to create an interoperable payment system that creates access for everyone and who are the key stakeholders?"

Joseph Chan with Financial Services and the Treasury of Hong Kong, China began by noting that among the objectives in Hong Kong, China in promoting the development of payment systems, was financial inclusion. "We wanted to assure our general public and small and medium-sized enterprises (SMEs) have access to basic banking and financial services," he said.

The regulatory framework in Hong Kong, China enhances the safety and soundness of (operations) and thereby strengthens public confidence in using products and services. The Hong Kong Monetary Authority, with significant responsibility for this task, takes a risk-based and supervisory technology approach, he said.

The other regulatory regime "we have is for virtual banks," he said. "Only at the beginning of this year we started to (offer) virtual bank licenses in Hong Kong, China (and) we have granted eight." The objectives of the licenses are to facilitate technology development, to offer better customer service, and to promote financial inclusion. From our perspective we need to balance financial innovation and risk management."

Hong Kong, China recently launched what it calls the Faster Payment System. The system connects banks and stored value facilities (e-wallets), enabling instant payments in Hong Kong, China, providing consumers and merchants a safe, efficient, and widely accessible fund transfer service 24/7. It offers individuals and businesses to make payments in multiple currencies—Hong Kong dollar and renminbi—in real time. "Basically, if you pick up a phone and input your friend's mobile number or email it will show the bank accounts or even the accounts available for that individual. You can then choose and do a payment transaction immediately."

"At the moment in Hong Kong, China there are 23 banks and 11 (stored value operators) who have signed up to this financial infrastructure and altogether 3.5 million proxy ID registrations. With about 7 million people in Hong Kong, China that is a pretty high penetration," he said.

Sang-seung Oh of the Korea Financial Telecommunications and Clearings Institute zeroed in on the developing country experience in establishing the needed infrastructure for interoperable payments. His country has taken a role in advising countries on doing so after its own successful experiences in establishing that in the 1980s when the Republic of Korea was still developing.

In the 1980s, the Government of the Republic of Korea through its central bank instituted a masterplan for developing an interoperable payment system. In 1986,

it established its own organization, the Korea Financial Telecommunications and Clearings Institute, which has been building, operating, and maintaining the whole national payments system since.

He noted the experience last year of "launching an open banking Application Programming Interface system," which has been allowing wide participation on its platform. Its success, which on the first day saw six million transactions, he said was because of the well-established interoperable backbone payments system operated by one unique organization. "It can be a very good reference model for other developing countries."

Oh added that many developing countries do not have a good development strategy. They are focused too much on technology, such as blockchain, or digital currencies, and not enough on the basic infrastructure needed to get there. Moreover, "many developing countries let the market do the job. They leave everything to the invisible hand of the market. We have seen enough cases of market failure."

"The most important and serious challenge for the government. . . is providing infrastructure to the people and, likewise, for the financial market," he said. He noted that among the five types of foundational market infrastructure according to principles set out by the Bank for International Settlements, the first is the payment system. "I think they put that first because they think it is the most basic financial market infrastructure for financial market inclusion. I think the government has that responsibility."

Richa Pant, of L&T Financial Services in India, a nonbank financial corporation based in Mumbai, India, brought a more direct experience from a developing country to the panel. She looked at the experience of establishing crucial digital literacy programs for efforts to go digital be more successful. "Part of our initiative was a digital literacy program that we co-created with our implementing partners. It identified rural women and trained them in digital financial literacy and then provided these women with tablets and had them teach financial literacy at the household level in their own villages. It is now operating in five states and has 650 such women. We chose women because we knew that if (a woman) would be educated she would be able to educate all community members and ensure adoption. We've reached about 200,000 people."

In India, unified payment interface (UPI) has been a game changer, she said. The Jan Dhan, Aadhar and Mobile (JAM) trinity is the infrastructure on which UPI runs, the two-factor authentication is being widely used in tier 1, 2, and 3 towns, however, through rural women "whom we call Digital Sakhis at L&T finance. We are ensuring that even in villages we are able to promote the use of digital finance." Where banks are at a distance use of digital finance, especially UPI, which is extremely easy to use and secure, ensures financial inclusion. Sitting at home a community can access bank, utility payments, remittances and even pay the equated monthly installment of loans via digital modes."

One of the key challenges in India, where government programs have had success in bringing accounts to almost all Indians, "was that even though accounts (were) in place many of them were not being used. So, you have about 95% of people with bank accounts, but not many being used. Nonetheless, mindsets do take time to change. There is also a need to bring literacy to merchants to help them better tap into emerging digital services."

Cuna Weaver rounded out the panel discussion with a look at the potential for the sort of disruption that can allow a society to go cashless. "If we define disruption as entering a market and displacing established systems—and if we think about the established systems that we are trying to disrupt as the use of physical cash—then the challenge is really in reaching those who are underserved by financial services providers. Until we tackle the inclusion problem, we won't be able to unseat cash as king."

Doing this, she said, requires an appreciation of how financial inclusion objectives are interrelated, yet distinct from cashless objectives. For example, in the People's Republic of China, providers such as WeChat and AliPay have been transformational in digitizing the Chinese economy. However, the country has an 80% rate of financial inclusion, so these apps could link to existing bank accounts. In other markets such as Indonesia and the Philippines, who have less than 50% of adults with formal accounts, the barriers to going cashless are much greater because people must first have access to an account before they can transact digitally.

"To convert from cash to digital, digital has to feel faster, easier, and cheaper than cash," she said. People want a seamless experience, not necessarily digital payments, per se. So to be disruptive means getting the user experience right." It is in this context that having in place the "rails on which payments ride" is important. That is, it is the infrastructure for real-time, interoperable payments that will allow the development of digital services which will convince people to switch to digital from cash.

She added that the system needs to include as wide a range of digital financial services providers and participants as possible. This means not just banks and mobile money providers, but also other financial institutions that in most markets are excluded from the national payment system, like microfinance institutions, credit unions, and savings and loans cooperatives. These institutions reach those at the base of the pyramid, she said. "And by doing so, (this) can have a significant impact on the uptake of digital financial services."

Enabling a shift away from cash thus calls for putting in place a real time payment system that allows other products and services to be "layered on top."

Brave New Lending: The Promise of Alternative Credit Scoring Models and Lending Platforms

MODERATOR:
Charlene Bachman, Director of Customer Success, Software Group

PANELISTS:
Simone Colombara, Managing Director, CRIF Philippines

Allison Howells, Head of Central Product Development Team, Experian Asia Pacific

Angelo Madrid, Country Manager, Tala, Philippines

Naoyuki Yoshino, Dean, Asian Development Bank Institute

A rapidly growing group of technology-focused digital lenders are putting the use of alternative digital data, customer needs, and advanced analytics at the center of their business models. These new lenders are also providing more transparent, faster, easier, and better-tailored financing solutions that today's increasingly tech-savvy small and medium-sized enterprises and individuals seek.

However, with the abundance of alternative data and the use of alternative credit scoring, there are new issues on which data to use, how to use it, and how to do this responsibly while respecting privacy and other important consumer rights.

Learn how new entrants in digital lending bring new complexities, risks, and ways of thinking about the financing value chains, as well as new agenda items for policymakers and regulators.

Charlene Bachman began the session by commenting that over the years companies have continued their commitment to the financial inclusions agenda to extend the outreach of quality financial services by improving efficiencies while not losing high touch with the customer. The industry continues to innovate and find new models to reach underserved segments by developing new approaches to assess customer credit risk and understand their behavior.

At the same time organizations are educating those customers and investing in financial literacy, as well as digital literacy, that is required to take advantage of the digital financial services available.

What are the most common criteria used in alternative credit scoring methods today and the risks associated?

Allison Howells, Experian: We want to use different alternative data sources such as telecoms data, utility data, rent data, and then thinking a little bit beyond different types of data sources such as Grab, Uber, and Gojek. We want to understand the different proxies for consumers, and the capacity and stability to pay back different types of loans, as well as augmenting our more traditional data sources.

We also want to look at data that is permissioned by the consumer, and is already validated, which puts us in a better position to use those data sources a bit quicker. Ultimately, we want data sources to be displayable, disputable and correctable by the consumer.

We need to always evaluate a consumer's stability, ability, and willingness to repay as well. Today's traditional model alone is flawed using traditional data sources, so there is a huge opportunity. For millennials and Gen Z who lack a transactional history with banks, these new data sources allow us to really start from scratch. However, we can also augment traditional credit reports and histories with these new data sources.

What are the key advantages and disadvantages of offering a digital lending experience for both the customer as well as the financial service provider and how can these disadvantages really be addressed?

Angelo Madrid, Tala: We wanted to make credit accessible, to reach the previously "credit invisible" population in the Philippines. With Filipinos spending so much time on their mobile phones, we are able to collect and leverage a lot of an individual's data such that "data is the new currency" to underwrite the credit risk.

Tala focuses on the customer experience adopting a mobile-first approach to its business. Our service is rapid, it is fast, it does not depend on physical brick and mortar presence. This provides huge cost savings that is extended to the consumer. A customer can conduct all business in the palm of their hands.

For Tala, this business model is advantageous as it does not require a high capex investment. We have over one million customers, but our employee base is only 200. This is a very efficient financial model compared to the traditional consumer lending business model.

However, given that those advantages, the disadvantages are market driven. People are not accustomed to mobile borrowing; there are hesitations. Trust needs to be established; this is not easy and takes time. Also, the Philippines is a very cash-based society. We are working with our partners, and more importantly providing financial education to our customers to progress on this journey. The original customer model and design was based on consumer research, but we also need to continually evolve with the changing needs of our customers.

Working with several different financial institutions, how have the alternative lending platforms achieved a reasonable rate of nonperforming loans compared to other providers in the market?

Simone Colombara, CRIF: CRIF is a global company specializing in the development and management of

credit bureau services, and credit scoring is at the heart of what we do.

Our view is that companies using traditional or alternative credit scoring cannot reach sustainable nonperforming loans by credit scoring alone. This cannot be the only line of defense. Traditional credit scoring only reviews loan repayment data.

To enable financial inclusion, we can review the profile of an unbanked or financially underserved individual and compare it to the vast data in our credit bureau to locate a similar profile. This creates risk projections based on profile similarities. This is how we can create alternative data based on traditional credit data.

We can also provide our customers with alternative scores using other data such as psychometric data or telco data; the latter having a very wide reach of 80%–90% of the population in the Philippines. However, this information can only be used with a respect for their own limitations.

How are peer-to-peer (P2P) lending platforms establishing trust, and how has the risk of indebtedness affected P2P lending platforms practices? What measures are being taken to mitigate that risk?

Naoyuki Yoshino, Asian Development Bank Institute: Generally, banks are reluctant to lend to start-up or small businesses because of risks. In Japan, there are now two types of companies, crowdfunding and investment companies, that can assist these businesses.

In Japan, the crowdfunding model is supported by an internet company that sells the goods of young companies online, creating the trust to buy from them. Through this model these companies can generate more sales to grow.

Supported by the Financial Services Agency, the investment model provides funding for the startup and small companies, and a platform for online sales. These companies also receive consulting and advisory services as they grow to ensure their success.

In both cases, these companies' financials and any loans and repayments are being recorded. This financial information can be a bridge to a relationship with a bank, so in this way the startups and small and medium-sized enterprises are being supported by mitigating the risk of over-indebtedness as they grow their business.

How is the advent of alternative credit scoring models influencing traditional banks to adjust their credit risk profiles? What is the impact and outreach of introducing these models?

Howells: In the United States (US), using additional data sources we have seen increased confidence to increase loan approvals. Comparatively in Asia, we are still learning as we review new data sets. It is imperative to have an industry expert interpret the new data that is being sourced to confirm its effectiveness as a proxy. The context can be different in each market for similar data sets. We need to understand how these data sources can be used as a trusted source for underwriting risk.

How is an individual's privacy being protected as these non-traditional data points are being collected?

Madrid: Data protection is about informed consent. The company explains to the customer how the data will be used and for what purpose. The company needs to ensure that the data resides in a technical infrastructure that is secure and has appropriate internal controls. Tala goes beyond basic requirements to ensure that we have both a strong data and ethical policy.

On the regulatory side, there should be a feedback loop between the fintech companies and the regulator.

There needs to be a balance between the ability to innovate and ensuring respect for the customer's privacy rights.

When installing our app, it is the responsibility of the borrower to read the terms and conditions. As an example of behavior data that we use, we track the amount of time that a new customer spends on the terms and conditions page; there is a correlation between the time spent to review the terms and conditions and the repayment behavior. This confirms our observation that informed borrowers are better for business.

What infrastructure do you see is required to ease the adoption of alternative lending platforms?

Colombara: There are three areas that are under the control of the lenders, which includes credit scoring, customer care, and education to understand the practice of borrowing and making it easy for customers to repay.

A digital infrastructure that enables a valid digital identification (ID) and ensures accessibility and availability of data are crucial to the lender. There are several countries that are moving towards providing the facility for customers to provide access to their data more easily, while maintaining control of who can access, and what data can be accessed.

How can financial institutions leverage alternative scoring credit models to fulfill the credit gap specifically for MSMEs, and are these models different for this segment?

Yoshino: In Japan, there is no credit data for startups, so crowdfunding is important.

The Credit Guarantee Corporation was established to collect financial data from micro, small and medium enterprises and guarantee a percentage of the loans made by banks. By requiring that all MSMEs share their data to be analyzed anonymously, Credit Guarantee Corporation was able to create a scoring model for MSMEs, which has created greater trust by the banks to make the loans.

What are the success factors for alternative lending platforms to thrive specifically in the Southeast Asian market?

Madrid: More entrepreneurs are needed to engage in the fintech boom in Southeast Asia. Financial inclusion is a massive problem and it will take many stakeholders to solve this important issue. More Filipinos who have overseas experience should return to the Philippines to participate in the fintech scene. However, funding for startups in the Philippines is lagging, and needs to be increased to ensure the optimal impact of the fintech industry.

Yoshino: Crowdfunding has spread to several Southeast Asian countries. This is a platform where female entrepreneurs have had success selling their goods and expanding their business.

Trust is an important factor in Asian business. The crowdsourcing platform provides the opportunity for both the business owner and their goods to be publicly known and build trust in their customer relationships.

Colombara: There needs to be more outreach of lending in the rural areas, and engagement both from public and private sector to provide that lending, especially to micro-entrepreneurs. Technology can assist to keep the cost down of providing these small loans.

Howells: The emergence of fintech players such as digital banks have created a potential threat to banks, creating a knock-on effect of many banks to review their business models under the threat of losing market share to the new market players. We need to "take our blinkers off" and continue to take risks that have previously not been considered in the financial services industry.

SESSION 4C
Microinsurance: Expanding through Education, Technology, and Stakeholder Cooperation

MODERATOR:
Arup Chatterjee, Principal Financial Sector Specialist, Sustainable Development and Climate Change Department, Asian Development Bank (ADB)

PANELISTS:
Maria Mateo Iborra, Project Lead, IBISA sarl, Luxembourg

Brandon Mathews, Chief Executive Officer, Stonestep AG, Switzerland

Kumar Shailabh, Executive Director and Co-founder Uplift India Association

Microinsurance, barely two decades old, now offers life and non-life policies such as crop and livestock insurance with a high volume, low cost and efficient administration business model in emerging markets. In Asia, 40 million people have insurance coverage through their mobile network operator, where in 90% of the cases it is the person's first experience with insurance. While micro-insurance penetration overall still remains low, the high penetration of mobile phones and innovative technology applications is playing a role, and annual insurance premium growth is now greater than 10% in emerging markets.

Learn how technology is changing the microinsurance landscape, and how major insurance companies and regulators are joining forces to provide socially impactful, commercially viable insurance protection to underserved populations.

Microinsurance is nothing new. Insurance started with microinsurance, meaning when talking of insurance for the poor, one needs to look back to look ahead. Be it providing fire insurance for shops in the United Kingdom or health insurance in Asia, insurance for ships and boats in the People's Republic of China (PRC), it started with microinsurance.

In this panel session, Arup Chatterjee opened the session with this observation and then began to ask each of the panelist's questions.

He began with Mr. Shailabh: Microinsurance is not new, and it started with poor people at the forefront. We see this "behemoth insurance industry," which really ignores the population that gave birth to this idea. What are the gaps not addressed in a country (India) in which the modern concept of microinsurance was born in 2000, when the sector was opened? In addition, what are your views on the problem in scaling up microinsurance and why are our regulators always circumspect about innovation?

Kumar Shailabh: "The way I understand it is that microinsurance was a very top-down approach, in contrast to microfinance cooperatives, which all had a mass movement behind them. The trust factor may therefore have been a problem." We saw in the slums and villages of India that people don't trust people from outside but were very happy pooling risks (among) themselves. People were already doing a lot of risk pooling, people were already doing a lot of risk management together, and somehow buying it from an insurance company became a foreign idea.

In addition, perhaps microinsurance did scale up because when you call it that, it makes it seem exclusive. "If you would make it affordable insurance where anybody could have bought it, you would have seen a different uptake. I think if you want mass adoption, you have to come out with a mass product and don't label it micro."

He also cautioned that scaling up microinsurance must be understood in terms of impact, not just numbers. "Where I come from, it took me 14 years to work across nine communities trying to explain to people what insurance really can do. Insurance needs more patience. If you really want to work for whom we call 'poor' . . . you must really look at where their priorities are—not in risk reduction, but in risk management."

Turning to Brandon Mathews, Chatterjee asked: What is the real challenge you have seen in expanding microinsurance in different countries? Is it regulations or is it government policy or both? And does microinsurance make business sense?

Mathews: "Yes. It definitely makes business sense. Insurance globally is a $5 trillion industry. If it were a country its (gross domestic product) would be third after the PRC and the United States. So, a massive, massive industry," he said, noting that it is profitable in the long term.

He also stressed the huge impact of the business. Not only when somebody makes a claim for a health event or fire, but it is also (before that) the ability for parents to keep their kids in school or the ability for the merchants carry a little bit more inventory. "That's a huge part of insurance."

But trust is definitely a very important factor. "And I think it's because it's a complicated product. It is savings for events that nobody can really save for: I cannot save adequately for the worst-case scenarios." So, it is credit offered by an insurer: "They are lending you their balance sheet. And so typically they're looking at you in a microscope thinking: are you a worthy borrower of my balance sheet?" The insurer is taking your risk from you and putting it on its balance sheet.

In addition, it is not just one complicated industry. Life and general insurance are different. And so (regulators and policymakers) are facing a quite complex, large industry with a lot of money to do different things. "They (regulators) are typically underfunded, say in the markets where we work, where there's almost no insurance. And the regulator does not have so much money or staff resources to do their own work." It can be hard for a regulator to hear what policymakers actually want—whether they want to control the industry or whether to grow the industry. And without growth, nothing is going to happen. People will not get insured. "I think that policymakers can already speak clearly, but I think regulators need to hear what is really needed, especially in countries that have lower than 2% insurance penetration, and this is growth."

Chatterjee asked Maria Mateo Iborra what motivated her to enter insurance and what is the problem she wants to solve using technology in insurance.

Maria Mateo Iborra: "What motivated me was my father. I grew up on a lemon farm in Spain. We suffered some health (problems) and my father said he was saving because he would not take insurance. There were so many layers of brokers that in the end the benefits were so little it was better simply to protect yourself." She then worked in the space industry for 15 years, but in 2015 blockchain became a bit more mainstream and the technology fascinated her. She created a company to provide services and consultancy to industries that lacked banking and insurance and learned about all the challenges that insurance companies had in providing microinsurance, especially in agriculture.

"At some point the loop closed and I changed gears. I wanted to try to use technology to break or to try to break some of the barriers."

Technology can change not only the profitability of the companies, but also the experience and the value proposition for the farmers. Today's solutions are not sustainable, are cumbersome, and the insurance companies will pay very late. "That's why there is no trust. Because a person can give you trust once, but not twice."

IBISA (inclusive blockchain insurance using space assets) is not really insurance, it enables mutuality—risk sharing. "Instead of transferring risks, we use a blockchain technology to automatically take care of the back office of traditional insurance and to bring trust in one single ledger and immutability of blockchain. The company uses space-based Earth-observation data to build risk models and to do automated loss assessment. We don't wait for claims. Every month we do an assessment based on an index. And if there is a loss that can be observed from space, we do a partial payment, meaning that in the second month of the season in which the vegetation is not growing, the farmer will receive a partial compensation. They can then do a second sowing, or they can have food security." This will establish trust, she said, because they will see that the product works without having to wait 18 or 24 months to realize that insurance protection works.

The session then took questions:

Can microinsurance be the first product for financial inclusion. If so, which solution and how does one package it?

Mathews: "I don't think insurance is the right first product for financial inclusion." The first, he said, is a payment gateway to make collections in small units. "I know in the mutual model it may be a bit different.

But from my commercial side, where we work with mobile wallets, mobile operators, the payment gateway comes first."

Shailabh added that "credit is the most demanded product." Microinsurance should be a product that is offered. But he reiterated that "calling it micro kills it." When you are talking about insurance, you also want to grow with your customers. "So, we might have started with something very small, but as members get in, that's how mutual started. Mutual has a 300-year history. They did not become $200 billion companies overnight. It was 200, 300 years of history."

Health comes first. "Because if health does not work out for you, whatever you have, can be lost. That's something that we have learned from our members. Second comes life. We were a little astonished: we thought life would be first, but in our surveys with our members, we found health to be the topmost priority." How to package it? "I think if you sell insurance only for hospitalization claims, it won't work. We started this program primarily to answer the question what happens to my money if we don't fall ill. If your package does not include anything beyond hospitalization, there are very slim chances that you will succeed, unless it is completely bundled in."

Mateo Iborra: Financial inclusion is a holistic thing and it comes also with education. So, microinsurance should not be the first product. "But it should be a package that goes with education, last mile, like how you pay."

SPECIAL EVENT
Digital Marketplace

The Digital Finance Marketplace provided forum participants with the opportunity to connect with fintech companies and learn about the solutions available in the market. The Marketplace is a highly interactive session in which participants move from one station to another for a short presentation followed by Q&A. During the allotted time participants could attend 3 of the 10 stations of greatest interest and applicability to them, creating an intimate space for networking, genuine dialogue, and knowledge exchange.

Participating companies:
1. Digizen
2. Grape City
3. Korea Financial Telecommunications & Clearings Institute (KFTC)
4. MakerDAO
5. Nucleus Software
6. Oradian
7. Softgen
8. Software Group
9. CRIF
10. Vizor

KEYNOTE OPENING
The Fine Balance Between Risk and Innovation: East Africa Experience

Nick Hughes OBE, Co-founder of M-Kopa and "Father" of M-Pesa

In his Keynote address on balancing risk and innovation, Nick Hughes highlighted three key areas of focus. First, that the digital world enables the re-design of financial services. Second, that digital finance will blur real economy sector boundaries. Third, risks will need to be addressed along the way.

To illustrate these messages, he referenced two services in East Africa: M-Pesa, Safaricom's mobile money platform, and M-Kopa, which provides a home solar power system through affordable financing.

Launched in 2007, M-Pesa in Kenya today has over 29 million accounts, $740 million in annual revenue, and represents 30% of Safaricom's 2018-19 revenue. This mobile money platform has helped people by improving financial resilience and dealing with financial shock. It is estimated that M-Pesa has enabled about 185,000 women to shift occupation from farming to retail and reduced extreme poverty in Kenya by 2%.

With M-Pesa's humble start as a system built to enable microfinance institution borrowers to repay their loans by mobile phone, financed by a grant from the Government of the United Kingdom, its evolution has seen an amazing trajectory over the years. It is an excellent example of *how the digital world can enable the re-design of financial services*. M-Pesa demonstrates what can be learned from innovation and experimentation, and importantly, observing and reacting to customer behavior and needs.

Hughes admitted that M-Pesa's original business case was wrong. A very complicated microfinance platform was built to facilitate loan repayments for microfinance institution customers. However, based on customer behavior, what the customer really wanted was a means to conveniently make payments to each other through peer-to-peer (P2P) payments by mobile phone. When M-Pesa's P2P service was officially launched with

an m-wallet, millions of people registered in the first 18 months.

Important to the M-Pesa evolution was also the confidence from the Central Bank of Kenya that the m-wallet and payments service was safe, and customer funds were protected. From the beginning, M-Pesa's customer funds have been held in a bank account by a holding company. Safaricom does not touch the funds, and revenue is earned from transaction fees, not interest on the deposits.

Over time, other M-Pesa services have been added such as international remittances, bill payments, and access of funds via ATMs, as well as bank partnerships. Today, M-Pesa is based around the smartphone, via the M-Pesa App, and has created a truly mobile commerce ecosystem in Kenya.

The second point on risk and innovation—*that digital finance will blur real economy sector boundaries*—can be illustrated by M-Kopa, a word that means "to borrow." Hughes stressed that we need to keep experimenting and innovating. M-Kopa is an example of access to energy through microfinancing.

Today, around 600 million people lack access to electricity across Africa. It is estimated that each home spends about 50 cents a day on kerosene, paraffin or battery charging. M-Kopa embeds mobile connectivity into solar hardware equipment enabling a service that allows an individual to buy a solar energy system— purchase of an asset—through microfinancing.

While the move to a solar energy system represents an important shift to clean energy, M-Pesa's underlying microfinancing business model importantly provides for further access to credit. Once an individual repays the loan for the solar energy system, they have an asset that can be used as collateral for further borrowing for items such as school fees, a water tank, or fertilizer. M-Kopa estimates that each household may attract $1,000 in total financing; the company always maintains connectivity with the energy asset, and so can turn off the solar power to manage risk in the case of non-payment of loans.

Today M-Kopa has around 850,000 customers. The company first launched in Kenya, has expanded to Uganda, and has plans to expand further in Africa. Through their cloud-based fintech platform they can gain customer insights from data on a real-time basis, and through machine learning can even predict when the long-life battery in the solar equipment will fail to assist the customer with battery replacement planning.

In summary, M-Kopa provides a low-cost clean energy product, but at the heart of the service is access to microfinancing.

In speaking on the third point of managing risk and innovation, Hughes reminded that *risks need to be addressed along the way.* He highlighted that companies needed to be clear from the start about the customer problem that they are solving. He felt strongly that if a company cannot state its business case in one sentence then they do not understand the problem they are trying to solve.

In the case of M-Pesa, it provides a P2P mobile payment service that provides a secure, quick and low-cost payment solution. On M-Kopa, it displaces kerosene costs and a "dirty" energy solution allowing a person to buy a clean energy asset.

On the topic of risk, Hughes highlighted a few examples of risks and challenges experienced by the M-Pesa and M-Kopa business models:
* A well-functioning network of agents is fundamental to the M-Pesa model. There must be an interface for cash to move into the MPesa e-wallet. Today M-Pesa in Kenya has around 170,000 agents.
* For M-Kopa a challenge in the start-up phase was

sufficient working capital to buy equipment from People's Republic of China in United States (US) dollars and have access to local financing in Kenya. Ultimately this was resolved with a revolving credit line with a local bank.

However, he also stressed that across the fintech industry there are a few key external risks to consider and monitor. First, there is a concern by some regulators that easy access to digital credit could re-create the scenario experienced a few years ago when there was a microfinance institution bubble that created over-indebtedness in some markets.

Second, social media companies such as Facebook that have the customer base and reach, could be a significant disruptor in the financial services industry. Large social media companies could also acquire significant market players creating an imbalance in market dynamics. Third, there is a need for the availability of skills and people resources to keep pace with technology changes and associated risk management in the financial services industry. There is a growing need for data scientists, and a new methodology is required to ensure data privacy and data security, which is a critical issue for private sector and regulators to address.

Hughes closed with the message that it is imperative for companies to keep experimenting and innovating. He views the M-Kopa business model not only as a way to solve an energy issue, but also as a means to provide microfinancing on a pay-as-you-go model for other connected productive assets. He referenced the example that M-Kopa is now providing microloans for $1 a day to small retail owners to finance refrigerators so they can keep goods for a longer period and earn more revenue, an example of Internet-of-Things connectivity. Also, M-Kopa is currently conducting a pilot in Kenya on how to "lock" a smartphone with pay-as-you-go technology and financing services. Smartphones, especially for the younger generation, are a gateway to open a world of many products and services.

SESSION 5
Central Bank Digital Currencies:
The Good, the Bad, and the Ugly

MODERATOR:
Malik Khan Kotadia,
Co-founder and Chairman,
Finnovation Labs Private Ltd.

PANELISTS:
David Lee, Professor, Singapore
University of Social Sciences

Wijitleka Marome, Deputy
Director, Financial Technology
Department, Bank of Thailand

Marcello Miccoli, Financial
Sector Expert, Monetary and
Capital Market Department,
International Monetary Fund
(IMF)

Ouk Sarat, Director, Payment
System Department, National
Bank of Cambodia (NBC)

*Central bank digital currencies (CBDC) represent a
new form of digital central bank money that can be
distinguished from reserves or settlement balances
held by commercial banks at central banks. Some
central banks have started to consider whether
they might, at some stage in the future, issue digital
currencies of their own.*

*The recent central bank digital currencies debate
has been motivated by a number of factors including
general interest in technological innovations for the
financial sector, the emergence of new entrants into
payment services and intermediation, the decline
of cash usage in a few countries, and increasing
attention on private digital tokens.*

*Learn about the various design choices and
forms for central bank digital currencies and the
potential impact for financial inclusion.*

As implied, a CBDC is a digital currency backed by
a central bank and the fiat currency it administers.
As such, it would be used as a means of providing
monetary policy, as well as increasing the efficiency
of the system, noted the Bank of Thailand's Wijitleka
Marome, providing a definition to the start the
session off.

She added that, therefore "CBDC can provide you with
the same trust that you have with your currency . . .
(plus) it can provide efficiency in terms of settlement
and financial activities."

David Lee added that he doesn't "really have a very
clear definition." There is a lot of variance, he says. "One
definition people focus on is digital currency issued by
the government, with the trust in G, the government;
but at the same time, it is involving the wholesale
model, which is electronic payments." But the "crux of
it is still in G We Trust," the "G" referring to the God of
trust emblazoned on the U.S. dollar cash notes.

Marcello Miccoli from the IMF took up the point about
wholesale: "When we talk about CBDC we sometimes
leave out wholesale CBDC, that is CBDC that can be
accessed only by financial institutions. We tend to
focus more on retail CBDC, i.e., a form of digital money
that can be accessed by everybody, similar to cash
now, because everybody can hold it, bank or not, in
their wallet."

He also looked at "why" a country might want to issue
a retail CBDC, noting that no one has one single silver
bullet of the reasons why a central bank should issue
CBDC. One policy objective can be financial inclusion.
"It is a way of reaching the unbanked and the ones
who are actually underserved with respect to banking
services within the new digital economy. As such, it
could foster access to credit and promote growth."
Another policy objective can be to make the payments
system more efficient. In some countries, for instance,
cash is very costly to manage. There can be other

benefits related to the issuance of CBDC, as well as risks, such as financial stability risks and operational and reputational risk for the central bank. Each country has to evaluate its pros and cons depending on its particular circumstances.

To provide context, Malik Khan asked Lee if he saw any conflict between the original thinking—embodied in the original ideas of the Satoshi Nakamoto paper that conceptualized Bitcoin and its "peer-to-peer power to the people, elimination of the middleman, and trustless transactions—and the position a decade later of the pending Chinese CBDC called Digital Currency Electronic Payment (DCEP) and it's 'in-government-we-trust' context. Do you see these as two completely conflicting objectives?"

Lee acknowledged the first cryptocurrencies were born in the wake of the global financial crisis and the people lost trust in the banking system. It became "very interesting to think about how to have a peer-to-peer payment without central trust or third-party trust," he said, coming at the issue as someone at the time who was involved in manufacturing. With a digital currency, "at least sometimes during a crisis . . .the public could continue to make transactions."

But then greed took over and led to the speculation and volatility associated with Bitcoin. "The one thing that everybody (is beginning) to learn is that you must have a stable coin. When you talk about financial inclusion, you need to have a stable coin. "

The design of the DCEP, the design coming out from People's Republic of China, is that it is a substitute for M0 money supply (cash). "So, you tokenize M0 rather than going through government securities, which is a very indirect way of creating money supply. Then what you do is allow the banks, the tech giants and the institutions to use that as a stable coin. They can be as innovative as possible to retain all the (principles of Satoshi) traits of 'managed anonymity'."

With this, he said, you can design a system such that when trust is lost in the system, you can do peer-to-peer transactions offline. "That's the design thinking that the Chinese government has for DCEP. I thought that model was very interesting because of the underlying infrastructure. As such, with their stable coin, it is a lot more useful for financial inclusion, because when you can cross borders you can go offshore, and you still have certain control over your money supply."

Khan paraphrased: So the "DCEP model allows the central banks do what they are good at, which is managing systemic stability, underwriting, and providing the trust. Then allow the private sector, the wallets (such as M-Pesa), do what they are best at, interfacing with customers and providing the best consumer experience."

The IMF's Miccoli expanded on this theme, sharing details of the recent IMF Fintech Note to describe something akin to a public–private partnership. Noting the difficulties inherent in a simple CBDC for a central bank to manage, as there are operational and reputational risks, he asked "is there a way to reap the benefit of having a digital means of payments which is trusted, stable and secure in a different way?" An option could be: "This would be a 'synthetic CBDC', that is, an arrangement whereby private firms issue digital coins, but these coins are backed 100% with reserves from the central bank. The central bank in additions provides supervision and oversight. This arrangement leverages on the comparative advantages of the private firms, to innovate and interface with customers, and of the central bank, to supervise and provide trust."

The Bank of Thailand's Wijitleka Marome, meanwhile, noted that her institution is exploring the world of CBDC because technology was moving so quickly. Authorities thought: "how can we as a central bank be ready for this, and promote collaboration among the financial institutions." This was the genesis of Project Inthanon, a wholesale CBDC proof of concept project. So, we wanted to explore the opportunities and challenges of using new technologies in real-time gross settlement, with very limited scope, dealing only with well-established institutions in the wholesale system."

The NBC's Ouk Sarat sounded a similar theme, noting that his institution set out "to see what benefits this new technology is bringing to us in terms of allowing us to improve our retail payment system and at the same time allowing the customer the choice to connect with one another on a real-time basis."

The NBC's Bakong Project seeks to promote an efficient payment system and financial inclusion. It is a payment service allowing customers to transfer funds to one another across platforms throughout the country. It is thus a peer-to-peer fund transfer service combining e-wallets, mobile payments, online banking, and financial applications.

The bank was trying to create interoperability in a system that commercial banks, microfinance institutions, and others involved in the payment space. "We tried to link all these institutions to allow the customer to interoperate from one platform to another," he said.

SESSION 6
Cybersecurity: Managing Risk Across the Fintech Ecosystem

MODERATOR:
Peter Hacker, Co-Founder,
Distinction.Global

PANELISTS:
Katherine Foster, Chief
Intelligence Officer,
Sustainable Digital Finance
Alliance

Kok Tin Gan, Partner,
Cybersecurity and Privacy,
PricewaterhouseCoopers
(PwC)

Nigel Phair, Director,
University of New South
Wales Canberra Cyber Center

The next financial crisis could be a security crisis, so what do you need to know to be prepared and protected? How do you use your data and technology to reduce risk? How secure is your data on the cloud? How does human behavior change in cyberspace?

Learn about cybercrime, security and safety. Explore how to best secure your data in the cloud, and how powerful drivers such as anonymity, online disinhibition and psychological immersion, along with the minimization of online authority demonstrate that people can act very differently in cyber contexts.

Peter Hacker started with a quote from the philosopher Marshall McLuhan: "It is the framework which changes with each new technology and not just the image within the frame." He noted that this is particularly true for the financial services industry and for governments. It is vital to know as much as you can about the future.

What happened in risk incidents and cybersecurity "in the past," are very often not relevant for a financial institution or government, as the type of attacks are rapidly changing. Cyber risk has now become a real major stakeholder issue for financial institutions and governments but is often massively underestimated or not appreciated enough.

Hacker referenced a cyber risk threat initiative addressing potential global catastrophe scenarios for governments and major sectors. The Singapore Reinsurance Association was the incubator for the initiative's launch at Singapore International Reinsurance Conference 2018, but clearly honored its independent role as a representative of the Singapore reinsurance market and stayed hands-off in any of the bilateral work between Hacker and the subscribing (re) insurance partners.

The disaster scenario was quite complex as a review of a global distributed denial of service (DDOS) attack by ransomware in the form of Wiper (malware whose intention is to wipe the hard drive of the computer it infects) covering 3 vectors (methods or pathways used by a hacker to access or penetrate the target system). The study also included 8 industries including government and financial services, and 3 incident scenarios including power outage, cloud and domain name system (DNS) failure, and a combination of the three together. The aim was to look at the global impact over a 2–5-day period for the public and private sector.

Hacker noted that in the Singapore study, they estimated that between 359,000 to 776,000 companies would be impacted and emphasized through a heat map illustration that cyber risk today is a global risk. Looking at the various scenarios, such an attack could mean global economic losses between $121 billion and $234 billion and global insurance losses between $27 billion and $40 billion.

Hacker kicked off the panel asking the panelists what the biggest challenge for governments and financial institutions around cybersecurity is today. Kok Tin Gan responded that the biggest challenge is that there is a misunderstanding of the cybersecurity risk issue. Only when there is a better and collective community understanding of "what is cyberspace" can tackling issues around cybersecurity be resolved.

With a focus on the financial services sector, Nigel Phair responded that there is no "silver bullet" for fixing everything online. There is a technology and a policy component that financial services operators need to address to create a trustworthy and safe experience; input will be required from public and private sector experts. Each country needs to devise its own "rules of the road." Consumers also need to understand how to react and respond if they have a bad online experience. Phair concluded that we are living in the "new normal" around cybersecurity threats.

Katherine Foster noted that the dialogue on cybersecurity risk is limited to the attack prevention or response and that we need to consider risks that are being built into technology platforms and solutions. She noted that her work with global innovation centers, as well as conflict projects including refugees and conflict diamonds provided the experience to help build out vetting tools and frameworks for vendors and solution providers (including the Ethic Framework she collaborated on with Georgetown University BEECK Center and the Rockefeller Foundation). Sound vetting includes ethics, cultural and gender bias, team infrastructure, as well as consideration data and, most importantly, processes. In short, technology as an

enabler needs to ensure that there is no bias and risk built into the technology design that is not appropriate to the environment and expected outcome.

Gan highlighted that hackers are attracted to financial institutions as they store consumers' data on personal profile, credit card, and money, so there is a high enticement value to hack them. While big companies such as Microsoft and Apple will pay hackers to report bugs, hackers that discover a security hole (unauthorized access to a system or network) may not report that bug, awaiting a higher payment from another organization for this discovery.

Phair highlighted that there is a need for a "security by design" risk management approach. An organization needs to identify what the risks are, score them and create a control framework. Examples of control frameworks include ISO 27001, National Institute of Standards and Technology, and Payment Card Industry Data Security Standards. Using these control frameworks will provide the ability to drill down to differentiate the scoring, as an example, by transaction value.

Gan noted that the weakest link in cybersecurity is humans. People can be sloppy about how they maintain their passwords; many jurisdictions require multi-factor authorization as the password being the first credential is no longer considered very reliable. He noted the hacking of LinkedIn in 2012 and 2016 where passwords were stolen. There is a high likelihood that one's credentials are floating around the internet.

Gan emphasized that the focus of cybersecurity should not be on prevention, as this cannot be controlled, but rather on detection techniques. Again, Gan emphasized that cyberspace is something that cannot be visualized, so it is difficult to manage risk and make decisions based on facts and feasibility studies. There needs to be better visibility of cyberspace via virtual private network, the cloud, and e-mail.

On looking at artificial intelligence as a "friend or foe" of cybersecurity, Foster added to the notion that humans as the highest risk factor, noting that that blockchains have been hacked due to a user issue such as a lost password. Artificial intelligence can help improve the quality of entry points such as an iris scan or facial recognition but, again, bias and risk can inadvertently be built into these.

On cloud safety, there was a consensus across the panel that there were strong advantages when using a competent Cloud provider such as Amazon's AWS or Microsoft Azure. The cloud has cost advantages compared to an in-house data center, especially considering the additional business tools provided by these cloud companies. There was a strong view that storing data outside of a jurisdiction should not be perceived as a safety issue and given the high volume of data required for deep learning, cloud is the most logical solution given cost and speed.

Consumers' passwords were a discussion point. Gan described passwords as a credential to authenticate yourself in cyberspace, as "something that you know." He emphasized that with the numerous passwords that individuals need to keep today, it may be difficult to remember them all. His simple advice is to write down passwords, offline. Gan's preference is to use token security (a physical device used to gain access to an electronically restricted resource), or biometrics, but only with reliable and trusted organizations.

Phair held a different view on consumer passwords, viewing them as a flawed means of security. There is research now concluding that organizations that require employees to change their password on a frequent basis result in weaker passwords. Phair is a supporter of password phrases; only change the password when there is a concern that it has been compromised.

Looking at how the public sector, private sector, and people need to work together on this topic of cybersecurity, Foster pointed out that new players, such as Facebook, need to be better scrutinized. In her view, it is not just about the cyber and systems risk, but about the governance risk for organizations that claim to be doing "social good." Since its announcement, there has been great focus on Facebook's risk to banking on their now defunct cryptocurrency notion. But Foster noted there was little concern flagged over governance. She noted that we had some of the globe's most powerful social media and financial institutions defining "social impact" and "public good," the governance of which was covered by two or three small nongovernment organizations on their board.

Gan spoke about the quote from Jack Ma that "we need to love each other." While Gan believes that cyberspace can solve a lot of problems through advanced technology, such as health issues, and bring people closer together, at the same time we cannot get so distracted by cyberspace" that we forget about the person sitting next to us.

Internal staff is considered one of the weakest links in cybersecurity. However, Mr Phair referenced successive studies in Australia that concluded only one in five cybersecurity attacks were originated by an insider, while 80% of cyber-attacks were from external parties. Hacker noted that targets are changing, and Phair referenced the case of the Australian National University's unauthorized access by hackers. Rather than hacking to collect research and development information created by the university, they hacked the system to access personal data of staff and students.

In closing the panel session, Hacker asked each panelist to provide one key takeaway for the audience.

Gan responded that we should work together to focus on updating the regulations, as they are outdated.

Regulations today are established by a country, but someone wanting to hack an organization does not need to be in the same country. Cyberspace has no borders. As a result of this mismatch there has historically been no consequences for most hackers conducting cyber-attacks.

Phair responded with simplicity: create a strategy and create good digital citizens amongst your users. Foster reiterated her point on governance as a closing remark: cybersecurity is not just about strategy, but about good governance. As we are building out integrated new solutions, beware of the risks that we are building into our digital infrastructure and impact solutions, and the vulnerability that we are creating, whether unintentional or malicious. The unintentional risks could have a high human cost for the very communities we are intending on supporting.

Hacker concluded the session with his own set of key takeaways:

First, cybersecurity is a top minister-level responsibility and board responsibility. Second, cyber-attacks remain a real possibility, so each organization needs to stress test their capabilities from a defense point of view to stay on the front foot.

Third, over the past 10 years, there were roughly two billion new internet users. Digital accessibility creates digital, financial, and social inclusion, but at the same time more potential cybersecurity exposure with hackers seeking data, intellectual property or money.

Fourth, crypto technology is a potential game changer. Artificial intelligence and blockchain could also provide greater security mechanisms in the fight against cybercrime.

Last, no company, no government is big enough to solve the entire crypto security problem. Hacker firmly believes that the private sector, government sector, and individuals need to work very closely together to solve the cybersecurity issue.

SESSION 7A
Digital ID: The Answer to Speeding Up Know Your Customer and Transactions with Digital Ease?

MODERATOR:
Kelly Hattel, Senior Financial Sector Specialist, Southeast Asia Department, Asian Development Bank (ADB)

PANELISTS:
Alexandra Lynn Hollombe, Senior Vice President, Payment and Financial Services Risk, Gojek

Daichi Iwata, Director, NEC Corporation

Bob Reid, Chief Executive Officer and Co-founder, Everest

Bin Ru Tan, Chief Executive Officer (APAC and UAE), OneConnect Financial Technology, Ping An subsidiary

Who owns, and how secure is, a person's biometric authentication? Identification (ID) systems are crucial not only to know your customer (KYC) systems, but also efforts to improve financial inclusion in Asia and the Pacific. This session looked at the issues.

This session explored how digital ID plays a critical role in electronic KYC and payment transaction processing, as well as the evolution of biometric ID systems, and the exploration of an individual's ID and associated data ownership, access and security.

India's Aadhar ID system is the world's largest biometric identification system; each citizen is issued a 12-digit ID number. Aadhar has generated 1.246 billion ID numbers for 90% of its population, and there are 7 billion e-KYC cumulative transactions that access the Aadhar ID.

India is a remarkable example of what an ID system can achieve in such a large country, and there has been a knock-on effect of a rise in account ownership from 2011 to 2017; women's account ownership of both women and poorest households increased by 50%.

What is the landscape for digital identity and biometric information?

Bob Reid of Everest commented that systems are evolving beyond foundational identity, by including both biometric tagging, and more selective sharing capabilities with financial services companies that brings greater value to an economy and to the user. The result is a greater value chain being created by the evolution of the digital ID by linking with financial services.

He added that this is an important development and views India's Aadhar system, which acts like an operating system layer, to have greater significance when linked to the India Stack of financial services. He also views biometrics as utterly critical across the value chain to ensure uniqueness and human-ness, which is especially important in heavily populated emerging markets.

Daichi Iwata of NEC also commented that biometrics is critical to identify the person's "uniqueness"; this was the main aim of India and thus the government agency name, Unique Identity Authority of India. When a person enrolls in the Aadhar system it checks against the large database to ensure that there is no duplication. The other area is authentication; Aadhaar authentication is designed to verify both one's Aadhaar number and trusted data associated with it such as demographic and biometric details.

Bin Ru Tan of OneConnect commented that many countries still have multiple ID systems, such as Thailand and the Philippines, and there is no standard definition of KYC requirements across countries in the region. She noted that OneConnect's work with banks in Thailand demonstrated how each bank's ID requirements will differ in its KYC requirements; some banks require only one ID while other banks may require multiple IDs.

What is the role that government and private sector play in creating this digital ecosystem?

Alexandra Hollombe of Gojek commented that the company works very closely with governments to work towards having an easy, secure, safe, and scalable e-KYC process for its customers, such that customers do not have to go through the process multiple times. She views private sector interests as aligned with governments', which also want citizens to have access to many financial services systems and be safe and secure while transacting.

However, Hollombe noted that in working with the government all department interests need to be aligned. For example, Gojek Fin and Gojek Pay are regulated by two different Indonesian regulators with different standards of KYC to satisfy fraud and anti-money laundering risk. Gojek aims to unify both processes through its technical infrastructure, and views it as part of the process to create awareness with the regulator on customer experience and needs, and how technology is used to identify both the individual and the mobile device.

Reid added that his experience of having the ex-president of Estonia on his board has confirmed for him that it does takes political will at a high level of government to achieve a digital nation, and that partnership with the private sector from the start is essential.

Digital ID: An individual right to privacy and data protection. Who owns the data?

Tan mentioned OneConnect's work with the Singapore government on its central electronic ID for engagement with many digital services. Today a Singaporean can allow a financial services provider to access select information via SingPass. In the Singapore model, the government houses the data, and each citizen authorizes who can access their individual data. To achieve this model, citizens must trust their government.

Iwata commented that governments can build trust by their willingness to explain their processes and be available to answer questions. This is important as the new technology being used—artificial intelligence and blockchain—represent complex systems.

He also noted that, regarding privacy, individuals need to be aware and take control of their data as there have been instances where artificial intelligence has collected data to mischievously influence individuals. A system redesign is necessary for individuals to have clear visibility on who is viewing their data and for what purpose, so that each individual has fair and equal access to the market.

Hollombe commented that the topic of how to build consumer and merchant trust is essential. A core principle of trust is "You say what you do, and you do what you say." Trust needs to be built over time by maintaining this principle. Educating customers on what data is collected, why it is collected, where it is kept, and how long it will be maintained is essential.

She also commented on the need for regulators to have a clear understanding of the security and benefits for various data storage options, which is shifting away from on-site storage to cloud-based systems, which may or may not be in the home country.

She also commented on the higher risks associated with a data breach that involves biometric data versus passwords, which can be reset.

Are you in favor of an intergovernmental body to protect sensitive personal data? Do you foresee a global ID data bank?

Reid commented that he was in favor of an intergovernmental body establishing a set of global principles on digital ID with an underlying aim to support the Sustainable Development Goals. However, he does not believe any government should actually have control over the digital ID database.

Tan reminded the audience that there is still a learning curve as countries go through the process of collecting and using biometric data either by a central government body or at banks or other financial services providers.

On the topic of a global data bank, there was general agreement across the panel that ID is going digital globally, and there was strong and recurring view that each individual should own and control their own data, regardless of whether it is a domestic or global ID system.

Hollombe reminded the audience of the business models behind Google and Facebook by saying "if you don't pay for the product, you are the product." On the topic of a global data bank, she suggested that it is already happening now as individuals share information and give consent through terms and conditions on apps. She suggested that discussions with regulators and governments on this topic should take place now on how data is being collected from online companies.

Further comments and trends in digital ID
- From a tech viewpoint, iris and face recognition continues to become more sophisticated.
- In the future, individuals will be able to control their ID via a smartphone, with data stored in the secure cloud environment, controlled by the user.
- Digital ID become more interoperable across various systems.
- Social media is not seen as critical in creating biometric core identity considering that humanness and uniqueness are core considerations of ID, but it can be an add on.
- There is a move from two-factor to multi-factor authentication to mitigate risk.
- Voice recognition is moving into sandboxes as a means of standard identification.
- "Liveness testing" is a fundamental part of digital ID due to the high risk of fraudulent activities.
- The People's Republic of China is the leader, and Japan is already using face recognition for payments.

Suptech and Regtech: Creating More Transparent, Tech, and Data-Driven Approaches for Supervisors and Regulators

MODERATOR:
Douglas W. Arner, Kerry Holdings Professor in Law, University of Hong Kong

PANELISTS:
Joanne Horgan, Chief Innovation Officer, Vizor

Yong Tae Kim, Deputy Director General, Financial Supervisory Service, Republic of Korea

Peter Rosenkranz, Economist, Economic Research and Regional Cooperation Department, Asian Development Bank (ADB)

In a digital age, can regulators move fast enough to avoid the creation of technology-enabled monopolies by first movers?

Technology may not only prove to be an enabler but could be incredibly disruptive. What if advances in technology (e.g. quantum computing) create an unfair advantage for individual players? Could this cause significant disruptions to global financial markets? Could it lead to the emergence of a new financial crisis?

Learn how the growth of supervisory technology (suptech) and regulatory technology (regtech) are providing the tools for supervisors and regulators to keep pace with the dynamic changes in the financial industry.

After some brief introductions and definitions—which naturally alluded to the opportunities inherent in new digital technology, particularly as they relate to improving regulatory and supervisory functions—the discussion turned to the data requirements entailed by regtech and suptech and the role that new technologies might play.

In short, regtech relates to the application of technology for complying with regulatory requirements by financial institutions and by service providers to those financial institutions. Suptech relates to the application of technology by supervisors themselves, as Peter Rosenkranz explained.

However, this cannot be viewed in isolation. "There's an interplay [between regtech and suptech] and if you think about, for instance, [the] harmonization [of] data—a big issue—it doesn't make sense if, say, the regulatory requirements of regtech users follow one template and supervisors a different one," he said. A dialogue between the different stakeholders is needed, underpinning the important role of regional cooperation in this regard.

Once data is standardized, e.g. common data templates, then you can really leverage the benefits of technology (through big data applications, artificial intelligence [AI], machine learning). But "if you don't have the same standardization, especially for cross border payments, that's a bit tricky."

Douglas Arner took up that theme, noting that "when you think of regtech, it involves the use of technology for compliance, but also for regulation and systems design, because after all you can't really have regtech without supervisors." There may be regtech firms that sell their services to both central banks and to the private sector, and you call them something different depending on who the client is. "So how can we come up with standardized systems which enable public sector authorities to do a better job at achieving their objectives? Whether that's financial stability, market integrity, financial inclusion, or the sustainable development goals."

From a private sector perspective, Joanne Horgan offered that "sometimes there's a bit of a leap towards the buzzwords and technology (such as AI or big data), but you can't really do any of that unless you have good quality data in a standardized format first, and proper data governance around data modeling."

She elaborated on her thoughts, noting that from her point of view there has been a move away from high-level aggregated data into more granular data that is timelier. This is made possible by technology. "Twenty years ago, when we started [our company], we were really at that first stage of getting regulators off paper," she said. Then there was a move to online forms, with the use of Microsoft Excel and perhaps the application of data validation rules; then allowing different formats, different standards, and the application of analytics. "I think now what we're seeing is regulators really want to move to that next stage of using AI on data as it comes in, and not even wait two months, three months down the line, but what about using it upfront during the data collection process?"

In her view, therefore "there's an increase in the speed that the financial industry and regulators need to react [to]. And [an] increase in the data volume and variety—standardization is really going to play an important part in that."

Arner added that this is a process of digitizing data collection from the standpoint of central banks and financial regulators and thinking about how to design a system to better collect data and thus more easily apply analytics to that data, in order to better achieve regulatory objectives.

"I think there's a lot of potential with granular data, for example, and not only for regulatory and supervisory purposes, but maybe to start giving back more detailed insights to the industry as well," added Horgan.

Arner commented further that "from the standpoint of a developing country, when you have leapfrogging, it means that often you need access to new forms of data … and in thinking about those new forms of data, it is

an appropriate time to think about how you can design the systems of collecting that data so that it's most efficient for the industry."

The discussion turned briefly to some of the things that supervisors are trying to do in regtech and suptech. Yong Tae Kim noted that there are many areas regtech and suptech can contribute to. These include reporting—as mentioned, the automated reporting and the real time monitoring—and data management, market surveillance, misconduct analysis, and micro and macroprudential supervision.

"I'd like also to mention other challenges encountered in implementation because I am involved in the development of suptech…I think there are four main challenges to [activating] regtech and suptech: cost, liability, data security, and mindset. It is possible for financial institutions and regulators to incur significant development costs as well as ongoing and maintenance costs." Cost-benefit analysis, he said, is needed before actual development. In addition, liabilities can arise from erroneous data submission using suptech. So, it "may be advised to give some consideration to how to manage potential erroneous codes."

Arner then shifted the direction of the discussion to the needed strategy in moving away from paper-based or analog structures toward new technologies.

Horgan noted that " the tone from the top has to be right. If people are happy with [Microsoft] Excel…, that's fine. But I think what people often forget about is the maintainability and the future-proofing of systems that they're implementing. It needs vision and buy-in from the top."

Arner closed the session, which explored several other angles of regtech and suptech, with a final thought: "the technology is increasingly there to design better regulatory systems and better financial systems, but it all requires that we think about our roles, particularly in the official sector, in a different way. How can we do things in a better way and how can we use technology to better achieve our objectives?"

SESSION 7C
Fast-Tracking Fintech Innovations: Regulatory and Industry Sandboxes

MODERATOR:
Peter Lovelock, Director,
Technology Research Project
Corporate

PANELISTS:
Pieter Franken, Director,
ASEAN Financial Innovation
Network's API Exchange
(AFIN/APIX)

Callum Holmes, Advisor
to the Bank of Papua New
Guinea

Bram Peters, Programme
Manager, United Nations
(UN) Capital Development
Fund

*Regulatory sandboxes enable developers
to validate a concept that is either not
permitted by current regulatory and/
or policy frameworks or where there is
regulatory ambiguity, in order to demonstrate
commercial viability. By allowing
experimentation of new and innovative
financial technologies in a controlled
environment, unintended consequences
can be discovered and addressed without
introducing systemic risk. A sandbox process
enables developers to pinpoint specific
regulatory constraints; regulators can then
review and consider issuing amendments
or clarifications to permit marketplace
deployment. This approach reduces the
time for taking an idea to market, largely
because regulators can focus on specific
changes instead of trying to update an entire
framework at once.*

The moderator, Peter Lovelock, set up the conversation as a discussion between the participants conducting and setting up sandbox experiments, Callum Holmes, Pieter Franken, and Bram Peters, who cautioned that in considering sandboxes as a way to test new techniques, one should be asking whether it is really the most efficient approach.

The moderator started by asking Holmes for an update on where the Bank of Papua New Guinea is with its sandbox and what its focus is.

Holmes answered that, in short, after 2.5 years of preparation, it is nearing completion: "We recently concluded our final presentation to our executive committee at the bank, the governor, the deputy governor, and two assistant governors. In a couple of weeks' time, after a series of presentations on the fundamentals of the sandbox to the commercial banks, regulators, and others, the central bank governor is expected to announce that the sandbox is open for business."

The moderator, Lovelock, then shifted down the panel to Franken of AFIN/APIX.

APIX is an innovation sandbox and cross-border community of banks, fintechs, and financial institutions partnering to create disruptive technologies and cause digital transformation in the banking and finance sectors.

Franken said the platform began about 3 years ago and "came out of the fintech drive in Singapore, where a lot of focus was put on incubators. In this, he said, it became apparent that fintechs struggle to get their solutions "live" at banks. "So, we started to look at that problem and the bigger context of the problem," referring to the 1.7 billion unbanked people worldwide. "That is clearly a huge opportunity, but also huge challenge, with various causes."

"One of them is clearly bringing down the cost of the technology so it can reach people. You need to make products cheap enough so you can still make money, but you can also reach out to people. "Telephony or accessibility of smartphones over the last 10 years has dramatically grown, but access to financial services has lagged far behind in some countries; you have 100% penetration of smartphones, but 30% penetration of financial services in some countries."

The question becomes, he said, why are banks not moving fast enough, yet the financial technology companies (fintechs) are there. "If these banks are not going to go digital, they're going to definitely become irrelevant. I think over the coming 5 to 10 years that's going to play out unless you digitize." He likened this situation to that of the Trabant car of old East Germany, a car with a delivery time of 15 years and a maximum speed of about 40 miles an hour. "Now imagine you are in East Germany before the wall fell, you wouldn't know that there was anything faster. You wouldn't know that the cars normally didn't break down." Yet a lot of disruption is indeed happening in the financial industry, he said, pointing to the Grab story. The Singapore-based company, founded in Malaysia, after starting in taxi hailing, has moved into food delivery and digital payment services via mobile applications. Such companies are even starting to chip away at the bigger problem of financial inclusion.

"We did a survey among fintechs in Southeast Asia over the last couple of months and it takes typically 2 years for a fintech to sell a solution to a bank. Most fintechs end up not getting the deal after waiting for 2 years, and so on… because (the banks) want to see if those little fintechs are financially stable."

So APIX is focusing on how to accelerate the process between fintechs and banks. "It is a platform that brings these two entities together. In essence, it allows fintechs to publish their technology as APIs (application programming interface) and allows banks to come in and take those APIs and, on the platform which sits in the cloud, start building prototypes." This removes hurdles built into banks and can shorten the process to get things built from "a couple of years to a couple of weeks."

Peters comes at the issue from the perspective of an innovation hub, however. He questions the appropriateness of the sandbox approach: "Is it the most efficient way? Because putting a solution in a sandbox places big pressure on the resources that a central bank has. And most of the central banks in the Pacific (and some in Asia) have limited resources, and very often juggle with priorities and have 'bigger fish to fry'."

He began by first explaining what the UN Capital Development Fund does. Peters manages the Pacific operations of that organization through the Pacific Financial Inclusion Program, which works with a variety of stakeholders in the market to spur financial inclusion, mostly through digital means since 2008. "We work with central banks as well as the private sector, but most of the resources we deploy in the markets we work in are injected in initiatives with the private sector. Think of insurance providers, mobile network operators, banks, microfinance institutions, you name it. And in our work we try to nudge those players to be more innovative and develop products and services for people who are typically excluded or underserved in those markets."

In the last couple of years, he explained, his program started taking a different approach, working with incumbents in the Pacific markets by nudging from within. "We have quite a number of our private sector partners (in which) we've set up an innovation lab to develop new types of services for the markets that are underserved." Some of those labs, he said, have been quite successful. "Through this approach we de-risk investments and work with our partners to be more innovative and take risks that they normally would not take. It has to be said that these are not always successful and that there are also quite a number that have failed. But I think that's the responsibility of a development partner, such as UN Capital Development Fund, which applies a market development approach. We want to support private sector partners in developing more appetite for risks and nudge the market to be more inclusive."

Central Banks in the Pacific region, compared to many in Africa or even Asia have "very much an open-door policy. They're very receptive to innovation." That begs the question: "If we already have a situation with an informal open-door policy, then why would you fix something that is not broken? Aren't there better ways to use our valuable resources and look at what other policies we can put in place, rather than formalizing something through a regulatory sandbox, that is informally already happening."

Lovelock played devil's advocate: "Why on earth would you 'do' a sandbox?," reframing the issue for the sake of discussion. He turned to Holmes: "What does success for Papua New Guinea look like for the sandbox. What do you think success is going to bring to us with the sandbox?"

Holmes answered with some background:

"We ran this very first ever blockchain conference in Port Moresby, Papua New Guinea. About 240 people turned up—most were government department heads, trading companies, oil companies, and so on. We had speakers from about nine different countries. It was deemed to be a roaring success. In conversations with senior members over the following few weeks with banking and financial institutions all said the same thing: 'that blockchain stuff is fantastic, but we're not going to invest in it.' And I asked: why not? They said, 'because you can't tell us the rules.' When you can tell us what the regulations are going to be, we'll invest in new technologies, be it blockchain or something else. But we are not going to risk our banking license until such time as you can tell us what the regulations are going to be."

In answer, Peters pointed to a paper from Ross Buckley of the University of New South Wales on the effectiveness and the efficiency of the sandboxes versus innovation hubs, quoting: "... innovation hubs actually provide all the benefits that policy discussions on innovations associate with regulatory sandboxes..."

SESSION 8
Growth of New Entrants: How Are They Disrupting Traditional Financial Services?

MODERATOR:
Christine Engstrom,
Director, Private Sector
Operations Department,
Asian Development Bank
(ADB)

PANELISTS:
Rajiv Chandna, Head
of Growth, Business
Development and Strategy,
Grab Financial Group

Maria Gaitanidou, Head of
Compliance, Coins.ph

Seung Hyo Lee, Vice
President and Chief Product
Officer, Kakao Pay

Wimboh Santoso, Chairman,
Financial Services Authority
(OJK), Indonesia

*This session looks at several new entrants,
providing a window into the services
companies that are disrupting industries,
including financial services. The session
presented interesting ideas in several areas.*

We now live in a world, noted Rajiv Chandna of Grab, in which a 4-year old in the People's Republic of China (PRC) can be unaware of cash or plastic as a form of settlement in a transaction. This is a harbinger of the near future, as countries around the world experiment with new financial technologies that are upending centuries-old money practices.

He described his wife playing "shopkeeper" with their then 4-year-old and pretending to reach for her wallet and hand over cash to pay for a bottle of milk and the child is aghast. "This girl has never seen cash being used for a settlement in her whole life."

This situation, increasingly common in the PRC and elsewhere, will soon also become a reality in Southeast Asia, the region where Grab began as a ride-hailing service and has since moved into financial services, disrupting an industry at the forefront of fintech and the new digital technologies.

"I think, in large parts of Southeast Asia, that will be the reality, you know, in 5 to 7 years."

He turned his thoughts to efforts to regulate the burgeoning new fintech sector, noting that "what the regulators are doing, in particular in Indonesia, is recognizing that the world is changing and we are all on the same side and trying to work this out. I think anti-money laundering, customer data protection, privacy, suitable testing for lending products . . . are all critical."

He was responding to brief opening remarks from Wimboh Santoso, Chairman at Indonesia's Financial Services Authority, a government agency that regulates and supervises the financial services sector. Santoso noted that Indonesia, in developing infrastructure aggressively, is very much inclined to avoid restrictions on technology. "Transportation to Indonesia's 17,000-plus islands can be very difficult, yet most villagers have (communications) gadgets. With technology we can go there very easily. . . and thanks to government, they have useful coverage. One can imagine the possibilities that 5G brings and it will be in Indonesia very soon and will cover all the islands."

He added that in all of the new financial products, which can reduce poverty, you need to come up with a methodology or code of ethics to ensure they comply with the anti-money laundering standards, ensure cybersecurity, and so on.

The moderator, Christine Engstrom turned the discussion to the traditional bank financing market, asking "How are you seeing your businesses collaborate and compete? Are you seeing differences now in the traditional financial sector and how they are approaching some of your customers?"

Initially most traditional banks could not comprehend what our blockchain-based startup entailed, said Maria Gaitanidou of Coins.ph, a mobile-based wallet service in the Philippines. She said it takes a lot of time to gain trust. Everything is about trust and confidence and that there is "siloed" thinking that will never change, as it is a part of human nature. But what "we've seen is that there are many institutions who are extremely keen to collaborate." She said their Innovation, their growth, and their future relies on working with new business models and learning from that. "There's a lot of institutions in the Philippines that have embraced that." Seung Hyo Lee of Kakao Pay, a mobile payment and digital wallet service in the Republic of Korea, echoed some of these sentiments. "We realized when we tried to work with banks to enable the mobile peer-2-peer (P2P) money transfer and other initiatives, there were definitely strengths and foundations that the existing institutions can bring to the table and that's something

that the new entrants cannot replace." He said that his company has since been working with all the players in the field whether it's a newcomer or existing institutions."

Kakao Pay has a user base of about 30 million out of a population of 50 million, so excluding children and the really old, "you can assume that Kakao Pay does cover the entire population who would have income and have financial activities." That unique characteristic means the company can help existing institutions by bringing new potential customers to their services and products. For the end consumers, by presenting all the possible financial products in one place, "they can compare review and then decide what works best for them." The company is trying to bring every stakeholder together to create a marketplace or platform where individual strength can be highlighted and benefits everyone in the playing field.

In the dynamic session, the participants described the myriad ways that new financial sector innovators are finding to disrupt traditional business and offer better service for customers, while they complement these services.

Indeed, "I think the next generation of disruption will be all about partnership, partnership, partnership," said Chandna of Grab. The biggest competition in Southeast Asia, he said, is not other wallets. "It's cash. It's lack of credit history. It's small and medium-sized enterprises that are not digital. That's our competition, because that's true for 99% of the universe, 99% of the transactions." He noted that the competition "operates in the top 5% of the transactions, and for that to change it's going to be about partnership among established institutions, new companies, regulators, and so on."

Learnings from the Fintech Policy Toolkits

David Shrier, Founder and Managing Director, Visionary Future LLC

Money is flowing into the financial technology sector, noted David Shrier to start this session. Nearly $400 billion has been invested in fintech companies by venture capitalists in the last 5 years; "just in the first half of 2019, nearly $40 billion."

Moreover, new sources of financing are emerging that are not a part of the traditional venture capital and private equity world. "People are doing token issuance and raising tens of billions of dollars for blockchain companies without going through conventional sources of financing so we have really interesting and well-funded companies popping up in places other than Silicon Valley or Shanghai."

Giving context, he noted that upwards of 1 billion people lack adequate identification, that there are significant numbers of unbanked people worldwide, including in the SME market. At the same time, the proliferation of online activity is creating cyber-vulnerability amid new threats from aggressive hackers.

"We also see platforms arising—WeChat has over a billion active users and more than 20% of them are tied into financial services through that platform." Meanwhile, a lot of central bankers and finance ministers and policymakers are not well placed to grapple with how to appropriately regulate emerging platforms.

That is changing, however, as "we saw recently with the reaction around Libra." The response to the new digital technologies is getting more sophisticated.

In cryptocurrency, meanwhile, responses vary significantly, with the United States becoming more restrictive and the Republic of Korea less so.

This led the discussion to technology toolkits and particularly fintech toolkits.

"There has been some really great work done on toolkits (including) the Alliance for Financial Inclusion," he said, recommending it.

"We want to help non-technical people better understand these new technologies. We also want to create a pathway to applying that knowledge."

He went into a little more depth. "For the Commonwealth Fintech Policy Toolkit, we looked at artificial intelligence, blockchain, digital identity, big data analytics, digital financial services, and cybersecurity." The discussion that came up in the development of this toolkit was the issue of de-risking and how perhaps technology can address the de-risking issue of financial services institutions that are moving toward financial exclusion because they cannot afford to comply with current regulation.

It's a highly consultative process. It begins with some initial design and a consultation workshop that incorporates private sector, government, academic, and nonprofit stakeholders. It's important to have a multi-stakeholder view. "We want to solve big problems, so our digital classes are in over 130 countries helping innovators create new businesses and ventures. We put the books together to help support that as well and then work with a number of governmental and non-governmental bodies to try and spread the word and then bring the word into action."

Way Forward

MODERATOR:
Junkyu Lee, Chief of Finance
Sector Group, Asian Development
Bank (ADB)

In this session, the conference organizers asked participants to consider three broad questions and to break into groups by region to discuss their answers. After lively discussion gathered around their tables, the session representatives then shared interesting conclusions with the audience. The questions were:

What are the major lessons or insights you are taking back to your country?

How will you apply this learning when you return?

How can ADB work together with you?

Among the key takeaways that participants from the Pacific region spoke about were the importance of digital banking and, with that, the need for digital literacy including financial literacy. This echoed with participants from the other regions, with several noting the difficulties they face in bringing their poor and more vulnerable citizens to a level of digital literacy that would allow them to better tap into the digital innovations so prominently on display during the conference.

"This is a challenge we have got to meet," noted the Pacific representative. She also pointed to the importance of regulation and for regulators, including those in the central banks, to find ways to work with innovators. Regulation needs to make sure that it is conducive to the innovation that emerging companies are engaged in.

This tied into another important issue raised by the representative participant from South Asia, who stressed the need for building trust. "We have seen many cases over the years of banks going bust or fly-by-night fintech companies—regulators really need to step into this area. . . to build trust. Without trust, people will not adopt (the new technologies)," he said.

Similarly, the representative from Central and West Asia said his table talked about the regulatory and supervisory technologies discussed at the conference that can help regulators better serve their constituents. "Regtech and suptech can definitely bring efficiency in costs and time. So we need to work on that area," he said, noting that in economies in the region there is a lot of bureaucracy that could benefit from more efficiency through digital processes.

Most of the people participating echoed each other on the important themes of the conference. They stressed the importance of cybersecurity, a couple of them mentioned central bank digital currencies but said that such technology was a bit too early for countries in their regions, and they all mentioned the need for digital and financial literacy.

The Pacific representative noted, however, that each country is different and brings a different set of challenges and strengths to the table. This, the representatives seemed to agree, called for tailored solutions from ADB, to allow them to best take advantage of emerging technologies.

Also what is challenging, she said, is the infrastructure, particularly internet, that is needed to be able to participate in many of the emerging digital technologies. "That is one of the things we'll take back to our country."

It is important, said participants, to not only look at what new technologies are available, but first to look at what exactly are the problems you want to solve and then to pick the appropriate technology.

The representative from South Asia ranked his region's key takeaways as follows, echoing other participants:

1. **Creation of digital identity.** A fundamental for countries that want financial inclusion.
2. **Educating the masses.** There are different levels of education in financial and digital issues. Work is need in this area if financial inclusion is to be achieved.
3. **Standardization of electronic know-your-customer processes:** When this is not achieved, end users suffer.
4. **Trust.** Without trust, people will not adopt technologies.

CLOSING REMARKS
Diwakar Gupta
Vice-President for Private Sector
and Public–Private Partnerships

Ladies and gentlemen, it has been a great pleasure to cohost Asia Finance Forum 2019 and its informative workshops and deep dive sessions. The resultant productive discussions exploring digital technologies and the innovate ways for achieving more inclusive finance have helped all of us.

I know you are tired, so I'll briefly share the takeaways from the two-day conference. It's fair to say that the sessions yesterday and today offered some dynamic presentations covering the great variety of emergent technologies we can use to broaden financial access.

We learned for example about how to reach underserved and untapped markets at the base of the pyramid; that is, how to locate and then tap customers among the poorest and most vulnerable members of our society using digital finance solutions.

In another session, we listened to some of the challenges they faced, particularly a lack of financial and digital literacy; this is one major reasons that women and rural communities, among others, have trouble accessing financial services. Enhancing financial inclusion therefore calls for more active efforts to expand education and literacy in these areas.

The conference also showcased several pilot Asian Development Bank (ADB) projects that are innovating new solutions that have demonstrated development impact. As you know, ADB prioritizes broader access to finance in Asia and the Pacific in Strategy 2030 as part of our efforts to reduce the numbers of the "unbanked" in our region, a big part of an estimated 1.7 billion people globally.

The two days of events covered numerous topics of interest in financial services, with breakout sessions looking at areas such as interoperable payment systems, the promise of alternative credit scoring models and lending practices, and the expanding microinsurance sector.

We also delved into the potential for so-called central bank digital currencies and what these hold for our financial systems. The jury is still out on their efficacy for financial inclusion, yet a few central banks are considering their potential uses.

Another hot topic in these last two days has been cybersecurity. We learned a great deal about managing the emergent risks across fintech, including how to use our data in cloud-based services and reduce risks.

A further interesting session also looked into the great promise of new digital identification (ID) systems in our work. Questions including who own's a person's identity and how secure new digital systems for identification are, were explored. Digital identity technologies are creating opportunities for electronic know your customer (e-KYC) and fast-tracked digital transactions, among other things, that can lower costs and expand financial inclusion.

We also learned about the new players in financial services that are disrupting financial services and whether these can extend their reach into poor and marginalized communities. The number of virtual digital banks continues to rise and the tech-driven FANG group of companies—Facebook, Amazon, Netflix, and Google—are making moves into financial services.

Finally, special events preceding the conference looked into the innovations and investments for gender equality and leveraging technology for disaster risk management. Our Hackathon Challenge, meanwhile, generated several fascinating efforts to use digital technology to overcome the special hurdles faced in the agriculture sector. I congratulate Asenso for its winning plan to provide access to finance to some 760,000 farmers.

We at ADB are eager to maintain the momentum and relationships we have established here. We are very encouraged that we have planted the seeds for future collaboration. We have discovered that countries see in very different situations and we need to ensure that our responses are tailored to ensure financial technology is inclusive and solves real problems.

I have two suggestions for you to ponder. The first is that technology does not always need to be cutting edge or state of the art to be effective. So, if you look at the most successful companies of the last decade, whether Whatsapp, or Facebook, or Airbnb, or Uber, they have not invented the technologies. All the technologies existed. Whatsapp mapped the mobile number to an internet address. The others really opened up what you had in communication channels for about 15 or 20 years with a platform that allows you to connect seamlessly. Very often it is the innovative application of technology that will have a lot more effectiveness for the end goal of making lives better, than inventing the technology itself.

Second, even more important, execution is key. You can have a lot of good solutions and best practices, but at the end of the day, getting down and getting your hands dirty is what really makes it effective.

Thank you.